IMAGES
of America

BLOOMFIELD

The Plaza Theater was built in 1917 by J. B. Clark, Bloomfield resident. For the next 42 years, the Plaza Theater became Bloomfield's window to the world, providing laughter, tears, romance, and the ever-so-popular 17 cartoons on Saturday morning. In 1959, it was purchased by Immaculate Conception Parish to be used as a temporary church until 1961. Theater groups occupied the facility from 1961 to 1989, when it became the Plaza II. It went dark in 2002. Pittsburgh developer Marcia Daktor purchased the building and after extensive interior reconstruction, Starbucks and Grinders Deli occupy the space.

On the cover: The Plaza Theater is pictured in 1937. (Courtesy of University of Pittsburgh Photographers Collection, Archives Service Center.)

IMAGES
of America

BLOOMFIELD

Janet Cercone Scullion

ARCADIA
PUBLISHING

Published by Arcadia Publishing
Charleston, South Carolina

Library of Congress Control Number: 2009920833

For all general information contact Arcadia Publishing at:
Telephone 843-853-2070
Fax 843-853-0044
E-mail sales@arcadiapublishing.com
For customer service and orders:
Toll-Free 1-888-313-2665

Visit us on the Internet at www.arcadiapublishing.com

B. OF E. PAVING BET. TRACKS - LIBERTY AVE. AT NO. 4766 VIEW N.   10-29-17 5166

This book is a memoir for my husband and my friend Bob Scullion Sr., my parents Dan and Mary Damico Cercone, my grandparents Rachel and Panfilo Cercone and Katarina and Tony Damico, and my mother-in-law Dorothy "Tootie" Scullion, all of whom instilled much love for Bloomfield within my heart.

CONTENTS

ACKNOWLEDGMENTS

A book is merely a reflection of the thoughts and experiences of others put to paper for the reader to relive and re-experience again. To all of those who have entrusted me with their memories and part of their inner-self, I say thank you for such a privilege.

The kind guidance of my editor, Erin Vosgien, provided the necessary road map to begin this adventure.

I want to thank the following dear and faithful friends who provided the footprints in the snow to proceed down that road.

My gratitude to Patti Donatelli Fern who did an extraordinary job with her technical skills and provided careful attention and dedication in a loving manner about a topic close to her own heart.

Thanks for the indispensable proofreading of life-long friends Angela Piper; Patty O'Connor Ladasky; my cousin Karen Cercone, Ph.D., who provided the necessary guidance, wisdom, and humor; and my pastor, Fr. John Dinello.

Many thanks to my wonderful children Bobby, Anna, Danny, Dennis, Johnny, and Joe, and my brother-in-law Jack, for encouragement and support to complete the project.

To all of the following who will live in the hearts of our readers for time infinitum as they showcase their loved ones who have made Bloomfield what it is today: Bloomfield Citizens Council Board of Directors Ida Czarnecki, Jane Foley, Emil and Margaret DelCimuto, Phyllis McQuillan, Barb Zielmanski, Joe Covelli, Linda Vacca, Tony Sciullo, Jean Mazzotti, and Jolene Brozi; Bloomfield Preservation and Heritage Society Board of Directors the late Dan Berger Esq., Dr. Frank Santucci, Philip Ciarelli, Ray Fern, Dora Girdano, Pat McGonigle, Vinessa Turpin, the late Bina Shiring, and Ann Gleeson; Bill Reynolds; Marlene Scholze; Judy Koll; Dolly Frizzi; Joann Greisinger; Frances Sciullo; Irish Ignosh; Anna Marie Rainaldi; Ricco Maddamma; Judy Hoffmann; Jack Hoffmann; Henry Edwardo; Viola Madden; Josephine Vanucci; Dolores and Pete Fantone; Rita Turpin; Olga Sciullo; Larry Pannunzio; Tina LeDonne; George Caloger; Richard Renckly; Maria Ricci; Lena Caruso; Gloria LeDonne; Rose Carcione; Bill Kovach; Mike Schmidt; Rose Larus; Jim McHale; Diane Lydon; Frances Gasbarro; Angeline Sciullo; Orlando Scatena; Ilona and Bill Grenzig; Helen Lendl; Virginia Bruno; James Buckley; Adeline Ficcorelli; Augie Carlino; Elmo and Bob Buzzelli; Emil Lucente; Paul Sciullo; Margaret Gentile; Fred Macakaness; Bon Carroll; Ray Winter; Chris Winter; Catherine Spiri; Andrew Zin; Joe Reder; Bea Palmiere; Anthony Donatelli; Bernie Danenberg; Kathy Costa Fusco; Jack Collinger; Debbie Schimmel Nagy; Marlene Schimmel Joyce; James and Jude Wudarczyk; Kathy Dentino; Edward Helgerman Bloomfield Liedertafel Singing Society; Miriam Meislik University of Pittsburgh; Arthur Zigler, Louise Sturgess, Al Tanler, and Frank Stroker from the Pittsburgh History and Landmarks Foundation; West Penn Hospital; Kenneth White Pittsburgh Catholic Diocese Archives; Gil Pietrzak Carnegie Library; and Art Louderback John Heinz History Center.

INTRODUCTION

This great country of America was built on the backs of immigrants and yet, the stories that unfold in published history books have the same cast of characters and heroes. But what of the unnamed men, women, and children who crossed the ocean in the lowest galleys in cargo ships and later steamship lines, stuffed together shoulder to shoulder as a mass of humanity in the most dehumanizing conditions, leaving their homeland to courageously come to America? They arrived here homeless, virtually penniless, and speaking only a foreign language.

What a gift this country called America has received in human resources from other continents! *Bloomfield* is about their story from Germany, Ireland, and Italy. No longer will these wonderful individuals be nameless faces, passing like ships in the night. Their identity is in the following images for their children and their future children, to cherish and build their future upon. Bloomfield is truly a diamond in Pittsburgh's "crown of jewels." This modern-day community, once a Native American–dominated wilderness owned by the English-Quaker family of William Penn, had a remarkable transfer of ownership from 1750 to the present day.

Only three miles from the forks of the Allegheny, Monongahela, and Ohio Rivers, the highways of the day, Bloomfield had a very purposeful existence as the Casper Taub–John Conrad Winebiddle Plantation established in 1762. Crops would be grown and cattle grazed to provide food for British soldiers fighting the French. This tract of land was only one-half mile from the banks of the Allegheny River. The greatest battles for American freedom began in Pennsylvania and this area would be vital throughout the Revolutionary War as the tide changed and Americans wanted their freedom from the British Crown. Simultaneously, the Native Americans were engaged in desperate warfare for and against the French, English, and Americans as the New World strove to become more "civilized."

The heirs of the patriots, Taub and Winebiddle, would change the landscape forever by selling off large parcels of land in the mid-1800s. Streets and roads were named for family members, such as Winebiddle, Harriett, Gross, Mathilda, Baum, and Evaline when the Civil War ended in 1864.

Concurrently, the flight to America from European oppression in Germany and Ireland in the 1800s would set the stage for a period of rapid growth from 1864 to 1899. Bloomfield was annexed to the City of Pittsburgh in 1868 as Peebles Township and the 16th Ward, spawning the growth of churches, schools, ethnic organizations, factories, and businesses. Europe would see another exodus and Bloomfield would experience a large wave of migration of Italians in the very early 1900s prior to World War I, continuing through World War II, and well into 1964. As the 20th century progressed, a strong presence of community leadership evolved from St. Joseph and Immaculate Conception Roman Catholic parishes. Bloomfield began to strengthen Pittsburgh's economy and create its own neighborhood renaissance.

It was Bloomfield that gave Pittsburgh its longest reigning city controller, Eustace Morrow, another important city controller, John McGrady, and Mayor David L. Lawrence. Lawrence and his wife Catherine would continue to reside in their Bloomfield home on Aiken Avenue after his election as governor of Pennsylvania. Having a mayor/governor from the same neighborhood is an unparalleled historic Pittsburgh event.

Today Bloomfield is a visitors' destination, such as Pittsburgh's Little Italy, where every restaurant and food store is still family-owned and operated.

The photographs of this historic Bloomfield neighborhood are primarily from the archives of the Dan Cercone Collection. He was affectionately dubbed "the mayor of Bloomfield" by Abby Mendelson in *Pittsburgh Magazine* in June 1980. He was widely known as an international hair stylist, inventor, and a sportsman.

Dan was an Italian who migrated from Abruzzo, Italy, in 1922 at age nine with his mother, Rachel Ciarelli Cercone. Her husband, Panfilo, had saved money while working in America and sent for them to join him. The Cercone bonds of love for their church, their Italian heritage, and American citizenship provided a strong foundation to become respected contributors to society. Likewise, the parents of his wife Mary Damico Cercone, Tony and Katarina Santucci Damico, also from Abruzzo, Italy, mirrored the same behavior and work ethic.

Dan, along with his wife Mary, sponsored Italian immigrants entering America and sustained decades of leadership and philanthropy in Bloomfield and throughout Pittsburgh. They made a difference in every life that they touched.

Significant additional photographs have been retrieved from the archives of the *Spirit of Bloomfield* family magazine published and produced as a community service by the Robert Scullion Sr. family and free to the public. Robert Scullion participated in every aspect of the magazine production from its inception on May 1, 1990, until his death on May 14, 1995. He was a highly respected, very active member of the Bloomfield community who took the stewardship of Bloomfield as a welcomed responsibility. Robert was a retired Equitable Gas company employee.

Janet Cercone Scullion has continued to publish the *Spirit of Bloomfield* family magazine as a community service project for Bloomfield. Janet is a graduate of Duquesne University School of Nursing with a masters degree in nursing education and post graduate work in special education at the University of Pittsburgh. After retiring from Highland Drive Veterans Administration Hospital as a neuropsychiatric clinical specialist in nursing, deeply involved in nursing research, she turned her energies to historical research education and development. The *Spirit of Bloomfield* family magazine is one of the longest-running neighborhood publications, and has won several awards. Janet's architectural and history program for elementary school students was inducted into the Library of Congress Local Legacies in 2000. She continues to serve the community and Pittsburgh as a member of the Immaculate Conception–St. Joseph Parish Council, president of the Bloomfield Citizens Council, and executive director of the Bloomfield Preservation and Heritage Society. Janet also serves on the boards of several ethnic organizations.

One

PATRIOTS IN A
WILDERNESS FRONTIER

The year is 1750. Looking back, it has been less than 70 years since King Charles II awarded this vast tract of land to William Penn to repay England's debt to his late father, Adm. William Penn.

King Charles II signed the Charter of Pennsylvania on March 4, 1681, and it was officially proclaimed on April 2, 1681. He named the new colony in memory of Penn's father, who was known as Britain's "General of the Seas." William Penn called his venture to the New World a holy experiment as he was deeply committed to the Society of Friends, the Quakers.

Now the adversarial climate between the French and the English for power in the New World, compounded by the pivotal position three miles from the forks of the Allegheny, Monongahela, and Ohio Rivers, would strip the Penn heirs and the Native Americans of their vested interests prior to the Revolutionary War.

Tension was brewing in what would soon become the gateway to the west. Change was imminent with unrest running high, Gen. Edward Braddock, Gen. John Forbes, Col. Henry Bouquet, and the then-21-year-old Maj. George Washington were an active part of the trailblazing movement.

The cast of characters in this historic drama would include traders, such as Christopher Gist, who would ultimately become George Washington's guide, and George Croghan. Landowners Casper Taub and his son-in-law John Conrad Winebiddle, as well as Native American Chief Guyasuta, and the Delaware Lenni-Lenape tribe would also play additional significant roles. It was the era of the Taub-Winebiddle plantation. What is known today as Bloomfield was part of Westmoreland County until 1788, when Allegheny County was created. This time period would be the embryonic phase of the birth of Bloomfield.

King Charles II ruled England, Scotland, and Ireland from 1660 to 1685, during the Restoration period. A debt was owed by the British Crown to Adm. William Penn's heir, young William Penn. He asked Charles II for a land grant between Lord Baltimore's province of Maryland and the Duke of York's province of New York. King Charles II complied with the request.

William Penn (1644–1718) is illustrated in his treaty with the Native Americans, created by J. M. Moreaule Jeune, as he walked among them unharmed, demonstrating his Quaker religious philosophy. He purchased land from the Lenni-Lenape, Iroquois, and Shawnee. Pennsylvania was the Quaker province from 1681 to 1776. The first 100 colonists here were Quakers recruited from England by William Penn, who had no military ambitions. As frontier battles continued for the British Crown, Pennsylvania became the largest English colony in America.

George Washington (1732–1799) was a 21-year-old major in the Virginia militia sent by Gen. Robert Dinwiddie in 1753 to deliver a warning to the commander of the French army. Washington carried the message back; the French were there to stay. He fought against the French at Fort Necessity in 1754 and again under Gen. Edward Braddock. He moved against Fort Duquesne with Gen. John Forbes. As Washington traversed the land near the forks, he referred to the Taub-Winebiddle land (Bloomfield) as the "high ground three miles away."

A plan of the city shows the position of the forts, the home of the citizens and the public buildings, Col. Henry Bouquet's redoubt, trenches and foxholes, and the blockhouse, which is still in existence and was built outside the walls of the fort, midway between the Ohio and Monongahela bastions.

Col. Henry Bouquet (1719–1765) had authority from the Crown to issue military grants on the improvement of land near the forts or military roads leading from one fort to another. Bouquet granted 303 acres of land to Casper Taub to grow crops and graze cattle to feed the soldiers two years before the blockhouse at the point was built. John Conrad Winebiddle married Taub's daughter, Elizabeth, sharing and expanding land holdings of what is known today as Bloomfield.

COMMONWEALTH OF PENNSYLVANIA

WHEREAS by virtue and in Pursuance of an Order on Application N° *3746* entered the *third* Day of *April 1769* by *Casper Taub* therehath been surveyed a certain Tract of Land, *containing Three hundred and three acres and allowance of six parcels for Roads, situate about four miles from Pittsburg* in the County of Allegheny. And whereas the said *Casper Taub will dated 19th February 1771 devised the said tracts as therein mentioned and appointed, Jacob Bousman Executor. And the said, Jacob Bousman by an instrument in writing dated 3 November 1791 constitute and appoint Conrad Winebiddle his attorney to obtain a patent for said tract of Land. In Trust for the heirs and divided of the said Casper Taub.*

And the said *Conrad Winebiddle* hath paid the Purchase Money at the Rate of Five Pounds Sterling, per Hundred Acres, with the Interest thereon due, agreeable to an Act of Assembly, passed the ninth Day of April 1781, entitled, "An Act for Establishing a Land-Office," and a Supplement thereto, passed the twenty-fifth of June, then next following.

THESE are therefore to authorize and require you to accept the said Survey into Office, and to make Return thereof into the Office of the Secretary of the Land-Office, in Order for Confirmation, by Patent to the said *Conrad Winebiddle trust as aforesaid.* And for so doing, this shall be your Warrant.

IN WITNESS whereof, *Thomas Mifflin, Governor of the said Commonwealth* hath hereunto

This description of Casper Taub's land, situated in Bloomfield, in an agreement with his son-in-law, John Conrad Winebiddle, is dated August 26, 1793. This document entrusted Winebiddle with the authority to oversee 303 acres for Taub's heirs.

Two

The Birth
of Bloomfield

The vast combined land holdings of two revolutionaries, Casper Taub and his son-in-law, John Conrad Winebiddle Sr. (1741–1795), would continue to support the plantation and farming era within Bloomfield for several decades beyond the Revolutionary War. Their wealth grew with tanneries in present-day Lawrenceville and the purchases of more land. The Winebiddle marriage to Casper Taub's daughter, Elizabeth, in 1761, produced four children who married into prominent Pittsburgh families. Anna Barbara (1778–1867) wed Jacob Negley and among their five children daughter Sara would marry Judge Thomas Mellon. Philip (1780–1871) wed Susan Roup and had seven children. Susan was the daughter of Abigail and Jonas Roup who owned a foundry and a maple sugar farm. Kitty (1790–1877) wed John Roup and they had one daughter, Rebecca Baum. John Conrad Jr. (died 1859) wed Harriet Fitch Ingals, and Harriet's daughter was Evelyn Gross, and her granddaughter was Mathilda MacConnell, who willed Friendship Park to Bloomfield and the City of Pittsburgh. The Winebiddles created their own legacy in Pittsburgh.

The City of Pittsburgh was incorporated in 1816. The plantation era ended as the four surviving children, Anna Barbara, John, Philip, and Kitty married and changed their lifestyles. They eventually sold large tracts of land to wealthy individuals. One such person was Henry J. Lynch, who purchased seven acres of land from Harriet, the widow of John Conrad Winebiddle Jr. Lynch built his home on Winebiddle Street, a Queen Anne–style Victorian mansion that Bloomfield would come to know, in later years, as Ursuline Academy. He then built St. Luke's Episcopal Church on Pearl Street near Friendship Avenue in 1865, the first Anglican church in Bloomfield, now the site of the Cercone Village on the Park. More than a dozen huge churches and schools were constructed in this era. German-owned businesses and fraternal organizations were the foundation of the birth of Bloomfield.

The Civil War was over. Bloomfield was annexed to the City of Pittsburgh in 1868. The Winebiddle plantation and the era of patriots fighting on American soil would become history. For Bloomfield, like a newborn child, every day would be a new beginning.

After the Civil War, Henry J. Lynch purchased seven acres of land from Harriet Winebiddle and built an estate house in 1867. The Ursuline Order of nuns purchased it in 1895 for use as an exclusive private school. In 1993, it was sold to Joetta Sampson for a celebration center called Victoria Hall. After 10 years, the Waldorf School of Pittsburgh purchased it and it remains such today. Lynch also purchased land on Pearl Street to develop the St. Luke Episcopal Church for the Protestant Irish of Pittsburgh in Bloomfield.

John Conrad Winebiddle Sr., a revolutionary, was born in Germany on March 11, 1741. He and his wife, Elizabeth Taub, raised their four children on the Winebiddle plantation that would subsequently be known as Bloomfield. The mansion shown as well as the Winebiddle estate passed through the hands of John Conrad Winebiddle Jr. to his widow Harriet (Ingalls), her daughter Evaline Gross, wife of Dr. Alexander Gross, and Evaline's daughter, Mathilda McConnell, by the beginning of the 19th century. This mansion, transferred from Winebiddle ownership in the early 1900s, still stands at 340 Winebiddle Street.

In 1866, a group of men representing 20 families met at the home of Christian Seibert for the purpose of reorganizing the German Catholic St. Joseph Church in Bloomfield. A magnificent interior was designed with very few changes—note the canopy over the lectern.

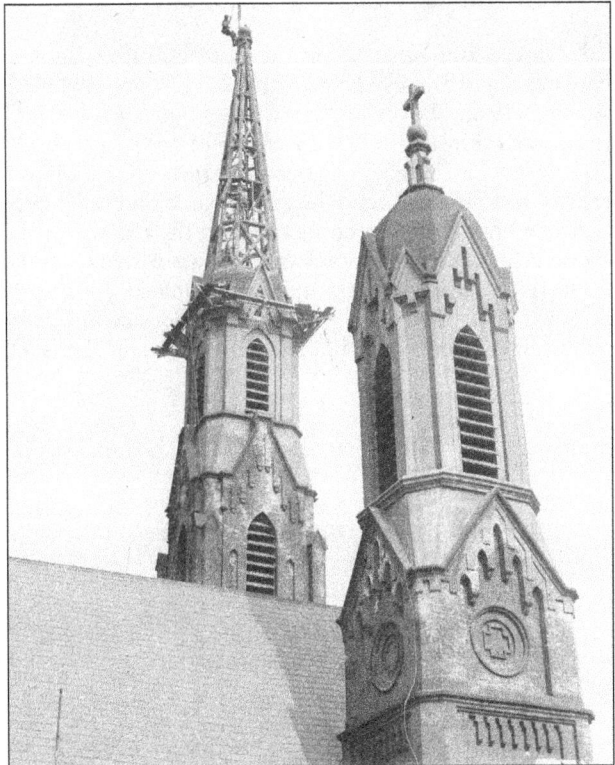

On December 12, 1885, at a cost of $5,700, the cornerstone of the present St. Joseph Catholic Church was laid. Two magnificent towers made it the tallest building in Bloomfield. In 1942, a flash fire destroyed almost the entire interior and forced reconstruction. The decision was made to remove the enormous steeples from the church.

The interior of St. Luke Episcopal Church, located at 162 Pearl Street near Friendship Avenue, is shown in 1992. The cornerstone for the church was laid on November 25, 1886, "with full Masonic rites," according to the *Pittsburgh Times* newspaper. Lodge No. 45, with 200 men representing 20 lodges of Pittsburgh, Allegheny, Sharpsburg, and Mansfield, was in line to march to the church at 161 Pearl Street. A school was later built on the lot behind the church facing Edmond Street. St. Luke Episcopal Church represented the coming of the Orangemen, the Protestant Irish, to Bloomfield. The entire altar, stained-glass windows, and wooden carved wainscoting has been preserved and restructured in the Bloomfield Preservation and Heritage Society Conference Room at 4727 Friendship Avenue. The Bloomfield Preservation Center is open and free to the public on weekdays from 10:00 a.m. to 6:00 p.m. Ethnic exhibits are on display.

Friendship Park Methodist Church, located at the corner of Mathilda Street and Liberty Avenue, was torn down to make way for West Penn Hospital's emergency room and Mellon Pavilion on Liberty Avenue in 1965.

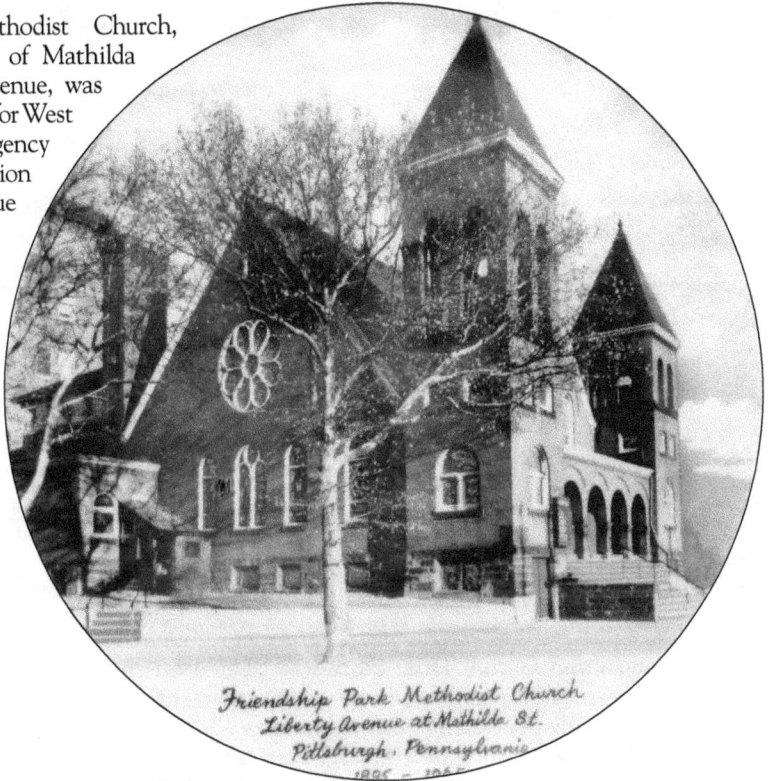

Friendship Park Methodist Church
Liberty Avenue at Mathilda St.
Pittsburgh, Pennsylvania

In 1893, the cornerstone of the Christ Methodist Episcopal Church was laid at Aiken and Center Avenues. After several mergers, the name was changed to the First United Methodist Church in 1968. Extensive interior capital improvements were made in 2008 to celebrate the church's 125-year anniversary.

The Emmanuel and Carroll Drug Store was located on the corner of Liberty Avenue and Cedarville Street. The Carroll family comprised several generations of pharmacists who resided upstairs of the family-owned and operated business. Today the fashionable Allure Dress Shop, a popular Pittsburgh women's apparel store, occupies the building.

In the late 1800s, three sisters, Catherine, Rose, and Sarah Hellstern, owned and operated this variety store, located at 4718 Liberty Avenue. In the early years, because Bloomfield did not have a post office, a postal substation was in the rear of the variety store. The three unmarried sisters lived upstairs of their business and raised and educated five nieces and nephews. They operated the store until the mid-1950s. It became Bambinos to Brides in the 21st century.

Frau Josephine Von Reinsberg Hartman, a very talented singer, donated the princely sum of $600, half to be used by the treasurer of the Bloomfield Liedertafel for bills and operating expenses and the other half by the singers to "keep singing alive in Bloomfield." In 1909, during the 25th anniversary of the society, Hartman was named as honorary president of the society and was presented with a silver loving cup.

The Liedertafel Singing Society Club has been in existence since 1884. It has remained at 412 South Mathilda Street. In 1897, the club, finding the building too small, added a second story. Later an adjacent building was purchased. In 1947–1948, the exterior was redone in stone. The organization will celebrate 125 consecutive years of social interaction and membership in 2009.

Mary Ryan Scholze was born at sea while her family was coming to America. She married Ernst W. Scholz II (1871–1948), a well-known bricklayer, in 1900. They had nine children who put down roots that lasted for generations. Great-great-great-granddaughter Marlene Scholze resides in the Gross Street home of Ernst III, her grandfather.

The Iron City Rod and Gun Club was a social organization that originated in the basement of the Scholze family home on 4009 Lorigan Street in the 1800s. They traveled as a group to other areas for fishing and hunting. Ernst III is the child leaning on the pole with the fish strung on the line. The club took its name after the city of Pittsburgh's title of "the Iron City."

Three

URBANIZATION, EDUCATION, AND BROTHERHOOD

The dawn of the 20th century would bring the Gilded Age to a close by ushering in the modern era and an urban lifestyle. The growth in church membership fostered a focus on marriage and large families. The City of Pittsburgh schools, like Osceola, Andrews, and Woolslair, would be in competition for students who could choose to attend the sectarian schools, like St. Joseph, Immaculate Conception, St. Luke, and Ursuline Academy.

The first settlers, immigrants from Germany, chose to fashion their row houses like the villages in their homeland. The increased population called for more goods and services guiding Liberty Avenue to become the natural main artery of Bloomfield, providing a direct, three-mile route to the point. The Greensburg Pike, renamed Penn Avenue, offered a road to Route 30. The Ben Venue railroad station, located at what is now Morewood Avenue, and the Bloomfield Bridge, built in 1914, afforded a real connection to growing downtown Pittsburgh.

Roads were being paved in place of muddy paths and streetlights installed. Bloomfield now had its own gateways to the east, west, south, and north of Allegheny County.

No less than 20 factories provided employment in the community. Among them were Federated Metals, Pittsburgh Erie Saw, Pollack Stogie Company, Drake's Bread, Straub Beer, Penn Raffia, Mello-Cup Candy Factory, Dean's Brickyard, Tech Ice Cream, City Ice and Fuel Company, White Linen Laundry, Peoples Cab Company, Norwalk Bearing, Mayflower Trucking Company, and Star Wafer Cookie Factory.

The first of two large waves of Italian immigrants would begin around World War I. Bloomfield was quickly becoming a true, solid neighborhood of the City of Pittsburgh.

Marie and Joseph Lendl were both born in Austria but met at a church gathering on the north side that was populated with German immigrants. They married on February 15, 1914, and are shown three years later with two-year-old daughter Helen and baby Alma. The Lendl's purchased Glock's Bakery in 1927 and lived upstairs with their five children Helen, Alma, Herman, Joseph, and Walter.

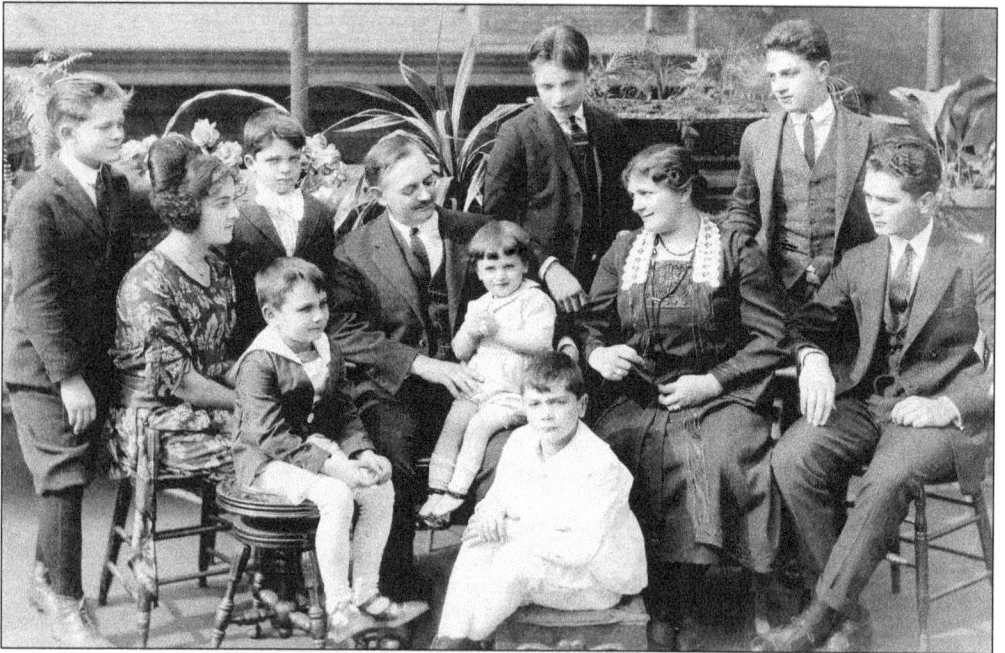

A portrait of the Christian J. Hoffman family from the 1920s shows, from left to right, Edward, Mercedes, Regis (in back), Richard (in front), Christian J. (father), James on his lap, William at his feet, Urban, Clara (mother), Vincent, and Christian Jr. There is an expression of warmth and tenderness shown here which tells a story within itself.

Madeline Fantozzi Dentino poses for a rarely done photograph around 1916. Her parents, Luigi and Marrietta Caruso Fantozzi, Italian immigrants, arrived in Bloomfield prior to World War I. Madeline attended Immaculate Conception School. Along with her husband, Murphy Dentino, they stayed as lifelong residents of Bloomfield and raised their children, Regina, Dolores, and Robert.

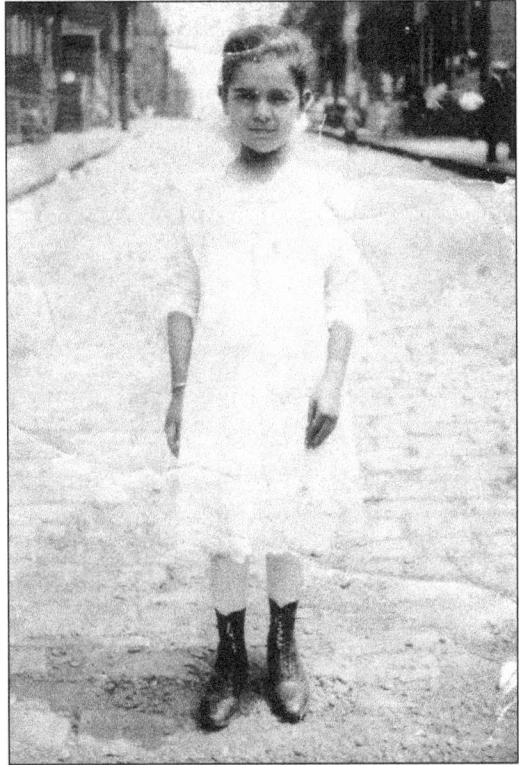

Nicholas and Lucia Frezza (changed to Frizzi in America) arrived from Italy prior to World War I. This c. 1908 photograph shows Nicholas, who died at 38 due to surgical complications, and his wife Lucia, who lived to age 78. The children in the photograph are, from left to right, Saverino (father of Sam Frizzi), Mary, Dominic, and Joseph. Their last child, Nicholas, was born in 1910.

Army private Dennis Roxy Scullion, wounded while serving in World War I, was part of the McDermott-Scullion clan residing at 4422 Liberty Avenue where his brother William Scullion had a barbershop. Dennis's wife, Dorothy "Tootie," was a very active member of St. Luke's Episcopal Church and a volunteer at VFW Post 278, while raising their sons Robert and Jack.

Michele Sciullo was born in Ateleta, Italy, in 1892 and drafted into the Italian Army in 1912 in the corps of Bersaglieri. He was promoted to major corporal in 1917 and came to America in 1922. His wife, Francesca Colangelo, followed with their children Jack and Mary in 1929. Other children, John, Michelina, and Adeline, were born in Bloomfield. They resided on Pearl Street.

Evaline Lutheran Church is located at the corner of Friendship Avenue and Evaline Street. The congregation was organized in 1872; however, on July 12, 1908, the cornerstone was laid. It took seven years to complete the building for the 1915 dedication.

The Liedertafel Singing Society Club began in 1884 and has remained at 412 South Mathilda Street to the present. In the 1800s, a wave of immigration from West Germany of mostly German Lutherans and Roman Catholics came to America to escape religious and political persecution. The strong German influence after the Civil War changed the landscape in Bloomfield for the next 100 years.

Rev. Joseph F. Bauer, pastor of St. Joseph Parish from August 1901 to May 1951, had strong interests in furthering religious societies and parish organizations. These groups included the Holy Name Society, Knights of St. George, Catholic Order of Foresters, Dramatic Society, Young Ladies Sodality, Confraternity of Christian Mothers, St. Joseph Social Club, and St. Joseph Casino.

St. Joseph Convent and School were photographed on Pearl Street in 1908. The first St. Joseph School was made of lumber and officially opened in January 1868. The earlier Sisters of St. Agnes were replaced in 1876 by the Sisters of St. Francis. The convent shown was built by contractor A. L. Huff at a total cost of $6,020.38 in 1897.

Rev. Florindo DeFrancesco, pastor of Immaculate Conception Parish from November 1938 to January 1951, was ordained in 1900 in Italy, came to America in 1907, and was appointed by Most Reverend Regis Canevin, bishop of Pittsburgh to care for the spiritual welfare of Italian Americans in Pittsburgh. Upon assignment to Immaculate Conception, he completely remodeled the rectory and the convent on Friendship Avenue that housed the Pallottine nuns teaching the children at that time.

The Immaculate Conception Church was erected in 1906 on Edmond Street and enlarged in 1925 after a fire. The right and left naves were added then. The land originally was purchased in 1905 by then-pastor Fr. Vincent Maselli, who served from June 1905 until January 1908. During Fr. Bonaventure Piscopo's pastorate, a chapel and school also existed on Lorigan Street at the foot of Pearl Street in 1910.

The Kenna family from St. Joseph Parish had five siblings, all of whom entered religious orders. The three sisters entered the Ursaline, Mercy, and Carmelite Orders.

The Hinnebusch family from St. Joseph Parish had seven members of the family called to the religious life. The three sisters all entered the Dominican Order.

This photograph of St. Joseph School's second-grade class was taken on October 16, 1913, on the school steps. The brick structure was built during the tenure of Pastor George P. Allman, who served from October 1884 to May 1901. The school was completed on September 1989 and contained 12 large rooms, a third-floor auditorium, and a finished basement to be used as a lyceum, library, and meeting and entertainment rooms.

At the time of this photograph, taken in front of the brick Immaculate Conception Church, the children were attending classes in the wooden building that formerly served as the church. Children carried coal for the stove in the morning and took the ashes out of the stove at night. There was no drinking water in the building. The year was 1929.

The lovely wedding photograph of Ella Alviani and Samuel Frizzi was taken in 1926. Samuel worked for Duquesne Light Company. Eventually they raised their son, Samuel Jr., in the middle of three row houses on Torley Street with Grandma Lucia Frizzi and son Nicholas in the house on the right and sister Mary DiCamillo and her family in the house on the left. They were truly a close and loving family.

The wedding of Mary Damico and Dan Cercone took place on November 26, 1932, with a big celebration at the Lincoln Turner Club on Cedarville Street. It was referred to as the "Grand German Club" and the only wedding hall of the day. Automobiles were a luxury then and events were close to home. The famous Four Notes band was hired. Attendants are Mary Colaizzi, Josephine Shusko, Kathryn Shusko, Charles Colaizzi, and Joseph Del Razo.

Emiddio and Beatrice Ciotoli Marianni's family is shown in this 1950s photograph. They were both immigrants from San Pietro Avellana, four miles east of Castel Di Sangro. Emiddio was a gifted tailor.

Angelo Sciullo holds his son John, age one, on the wooden back porch of their home at 215½ Pearl Street. Angelo Sciullo worked in construction while raising his son and three daughters, Albina, Caroline, and Frances, after his young wife died in 1939. Young John earned money as a shoe-shine boy in Dan Cercone's barbershop. He went into the service during World War II and returned home and became a professional barber.

This is a passport picture of Francesca Colangelo Sciullo with son Giocchino (Jack) and daughter Mary. They came to America on the steamship *Augustus* in 1929. Other children John, Michelina, and Adeline, were born in America. They resided at 421 Pearl Street.

Pasquelina Donatucci was Bloomfield's national treasure during the early Italian immigration movement. The mother of 15 children, she quickly learned how to speak English and interpreted for those who did not in all issues of health and death. She was a midwife, nurse, and healer, who found time to organize the annual St. Rocco Festival on Lorigan Street.

This J. L. Thomas family portrait was taken in the 1930s. From left to right are Gerald, mother Rose, father John, Joseph, John, Edwin, and Anna Marie. The J. L. Thomas Bar at 4648 Liberty Avenue was considered the sports bar of the day. Thomas was a great sports enthusiast. His wife, daughter, and other family members cooked in the kitchen upstairs and lowered the food on a pulley to be served in the bar-restaurant.

The Jones family members were a very active group of St. Joseph Church parishioners. Charles Jones Sr. did carpentry work and painting to maintain the facilities. Seen from left to right are (first row) Dorothy, parents Philomena and Charles Sr., and Kathy; (second row) Leonard, Maurice, Patricia, Charles Jr., and Raymond.

The immortal boxing champion Harry Greb, the "Pittsburgh Windmill," married Mildred Riley and resided on Gross Street in Bloomfield. Prior to becoming the middleweight champion of the world, he had fought Gene Tunney five times. Harry Greb fought 294 bouts over 13 years of his boxing career. He died at age 33 in an Atlantic City hospital on October 22, 1926, following a surgical procedure.

This photograph shows local funeral director William Winter conducting the funeral and acting as pallbearer at the 1926 funeral of boxing champion Harry Greb. Winter is accompanied by another boxing champion, Gene Tunney. The funeral mass was held at St. Philomena Church even though Greb was a member of Immaculate Conception Church at the time. Thousands of Pittsburghers came to mourn the loss of the famous fighter.

34

Shown here is a 1929 photograph of the Bloomfield Civics. Identified here are Rogue, Morris, Haney, unidentified, Shaeffer, Baure, Miller, Baure, Bull, Trozzi, Hunsey, Fehl, Caslin, Yount, Bartuneck, Baure, Flaherty, Eddie Cook, Titers Flaherty, Hughes, Dietrick, Lurey, Scholtz, Maulisi, Johns, Morrisey, O'Rourke, Schimmell, Thompson, Fuher, Besterman, Shields, Larkin, Lippincott, Dillon, Kelleher, and Haver. Ball boys are Trozzi and Fuher. The picture was taken in the rear of the Stracka Funeral Home on Panama Way.

This photograph is of the 1936 prewar Civics. They were coached by Charles Damico (left, second row), organized and renamed from Fleetfoots to Civics because "it sounded tougher" according to Dan Cercone (far right). The team played as an independent and posted an almost-perfect record in large measure to running back Gabe Patterson (far right, second row).

This 1917 photograph shows Liberty Avenue looking toward Taylor Street in the direction of downtown Pittsburgh. Note the unpaved cobblestone surface under the trolley tracks and flimsy three-light standards. The 21st-century businesses in that block are Thai Restaurant, Vacca Cleaners, Sausalido Restaurant, Lot 17, Dollar Max, and Tessaro's Restaurant.

This picture of Friendship Avenue and Edmond Street shows the Atlantic Refinery Company filling station that sat in the middle of the street. Terra-cotta was used as the building material for both building and roof. The other structure is the City Ice and Fuel Company. Cercone Village on the Park, the three-story Bloomfield Preservation and Heritage Society Headquarters, and a medical office building now occupies the entire space, including three houses that disappeared long ago.

The Straub Brewing Company occupied the current Shur-Save Supermarket property in 1913. It was sold to Bordens Tech Ice Cream Company and became a Kroger's store in the 1950s. Clothes lines strung with clothes flapping in the wind were a familiar sight before the days of dryer appliances.

Pollack Stogie Company of Pittsburgh was located on Mathilda Street at the corner of Yew Street and Lima Way. This 1908 view from Lima Way shows children in high-button shoes, a Victorian-era light fixture, and automobiles with spare tires attached to the rear. Pollack Stogie Company made the famous Argo Cigars. The building is currently used as an apartment building.

Andrews School, built in 1868, was located at 410 Ella Street near Liberty Avenue in Pittsburgh's Bloomfield neighborhood. The school was originally named for John Howard, a prominent Bloomfield resident. It was renamed for Samuel Andrews, who served as superintendent of the Pittsburgh Public Schools from 1899 to 1911. Andrews School closed in 1942 and was razed in 1943. The Bloomfield Recreation Center complex and swimming pool are on the site now.

The Andrews School class of 1931 shows students at the back of the building. Former students described hauling ashes away since the building had a coal furnace. A dump truck would also deliver loads of coal at intervals for heat. Only a few male students wear long trousers, but all are nicely dressed.

38

The Delledonne sisters, Esther, Elsa, and Ida, were 10, 8, and 6 years old respectively in 1938 when this picture was taken. Their parents, Angelo and Carmella Santucci Delledonne, had the painful experience of losing four other children to influenza and their only son, Angelo Jr., to cancer in 1975. It exemplifies the hardship and losses of families during the early years. This photograph was especially endearing to their parents.

This early-1900s picture, taken in front of Woolslair School, shows a group of students who appear to be very serious looking. Discipline was always maintained in the schools of the day. The shoes have metal eyelets for shoelaces and all are wearing knee socks. The Pittsburgh School Board changed the spelling from Woolslayer to Woolslair in modern times.

Dr. Antonio Bianco arrived from Naples, Italy, in 1919. He became the first Italian immigrant to graduate from the University of Pittsburgh Medical School and opened a practice at 4751 Liberty Avenue. He was on the staff of West Penn Hospital and visited the sick with house calls throughout Bloomfield. His brother William was his personal chauffeur and traditionally waited in Mierzwa's Drug Store for the doctor to call since cell phones did not exist at that time.

The Martzo Ringside bar, located at 4755 Liberty Avenue (currently Armand's), was a popular gathering place for lifelong friends. Shown from left to right are George Martzo, Bill Parker, Anthony and Paul Trapani, David Salvatore, and Tom Martino as they continue celebrating a Bloomfield wedding from earlier in the day.

Walter Raskowski played football for the University of Pittsburgh under Jock Sutherland and played in the Rose Bowl on January 1, 1937, when Pitt defeated the University of Washington before 87,000 fans. His speed on the football field earned him a scholarship through the university's dental school. During that time, he took Bloomfield's Mary Sciullo as his bride and they resided on Friendship Avenue while raising two daughters, JoAnn and Dolores Raskowski.

Pictured in Bloomfield in the 1930s are brothers-in-law Fabiano Maddamma and Emiddio Mariani, who married sisters Anna and Beatrice Ciotoli, respectively. The Ciotoli's and Mariani's were from San Pietro, Avellana, and the Maddammas were from nearby Villetta Barrea, Italy. Both families are multigenerational residents of Bloomfield. Fabiano Maddamma came to America in 1905.

Sam Carcione stands in front of his busy grocery store, well stocked with candy treats, at 4012 Liberty Avenue, directly across from Woolslair School. Sam purchased the building for his home and built a storefront around the large wooden porch. The store closed in 1957. It had been a regular stop and childhood ritual for Woolslair Public School students.

Ernest Scholze III was known as "Hank" to all of Bloomfield. He became a household name since he was everyone's ice and coal delivery man and also the Country Belle milkman. His wife, Teresa (Lacing), was very active at St. Joseph Church and a longtime bowler with the J. L. Thomas League. Their granddaughter, Marlene Scholze, continues to reside in the Gross Street home.

The Metropolitan Theater program from the 1940s shows movies of the day with features changing three times weekly. The theater was often referred to as the "Ranch House" because they featured so many Western movies. Not quite as modern as the Plaza Theater, two doors away on Liberty Avenue, it attracted more youngsters than adults, except when they had dish giveaway night.

BLOOMFIELD'S
METROPOLITAN
THE FRIENDLY THEATRE

Matinee 20c	Phone	Evening 28c
Except	SChenley	Children 15c
Sat., Sun., Hol.	4807	Tax Included

Week Starting Sunday, November 28th

SUN. and MON. NOV. 28-29	Brian Donlevy Robert Preston "WAKE ISLAND" also Jimmy Rogers Noah Berry, Jr. "CALABOOSE"
TUES. NOV. 30 and WED. DEC. 1	Fred McMurray Paulette Goddard "FOREST RANGERS" IN TECHNICOLOR — also — Don Ameche Joan Bennett GIRL TROUBLE" Dinner Ware To The Ladies
THURS. DEC. 2	Robert Paige Frances Langford "COWBOY IN MANHATTAN" — also — James Craig Bonita Granville "7 MILES FROM ALCATRAZ" Play "BANKO"Like Bingo Cash Prizes plus 2 Jack Pots
FRI. and SAT. DEC. 3 - 4	Susan Hayworth William Holden "YOUNG AND WILLING" — also — ROY ROGERS "MAN FROM MUSIC MOUNTAINS" Chapter 12 "THE BAT MAN" MONEY NITES

The Millvale Avenue Bridge is pictured on January 11, 1928, looking southeast. The bridge was built by the Pittsburgh Public Works Department connecting Oakland and Bloomfield over the Pennsylvania Railroad tracks as a faster route than the Bloomfield Bridge. The hillsides on both sides are designated parts of the Bloomfield community up to and including one side of Center Avenue.

Bloomfield's historic automobile row was erected in the 1920s. The Ford Building is at Baum and Morewood Avenue, and the Hudson Building, with three acres of interior built in 1908, has been a Mercedes Benz dealership since 2006. Sen. Joseph F. Guffy's estate and many Tudor-style mansions were eradicated to erect this building in the interest of urban progress in Bloomfield. Health care and commercial economic developers have tilted the automobile-row phenomenon. This building has since been torn down and a vacant lot is on one side and the Marriott parking lot is on the other.

Café Sam, another mansion of the very early 1900s, was converted to a restaurant on Bloomfield's historic automobile row. Owner Andrew Zin, a graduate of the Culinary Arts School of America, purchased the building in 1987 and named it Café Sam to honor both of his grandfathers who were named Sam. He has expanded the complete second floor into an outdoor patio and created a stylish visitors' destination, punctuating the fine architectural features with an exceptional dining experience.

Four

PRELUDE TO ITS OWN RENAISSANCE

A wonderful rebirth of the spirit of optimism and patriotism was kindled from 1940 to 1950. Bloomfield always seemed undaunted by events of the outside world, moving ever forward in the face of adversity.

Another dimension added to the churches for fortitude was fraternal and ethnic lodges, veterans' organizations, sports leagues, and political alliances. Dramatic increases in Italian immigration prior to and after World War II and continuing for at least three more decades would enhance the Pittsburgh workforce with much-needed tradesmen such as bricklayers, masons, and carpenters to supplement the renaissance of Pittsburgh.

As Italians arrived in Bloomfield primarily from Abruzzo, Italy, they quickly found jobs with building contractors, Equitable Gas, Federated Metals, railroads, and the City of Pittsburgh Public Works Department.

Businesses on Liberty Avenue would change hands frequently and more Italian-sounding names would be attached to the food establishments. Taverns were a gathering place for entire families and an important part of the social fabric of the community. The bonds of brotherhood appeared in every aspect of life throughout Bloomfield.

Notwithstanding all that progress, bicycles, skates, and wooden gigs (homemade scooters) were the main source of transportation for all of the children.

In this First Holy Communion portrait, Maria Balestrieri is shown with sons Thomas, on the left, and Anthony, on the right, and only daughter Mary. Charles, another brother, is not in the picture. The Balestrieri family, Sicilian immigrants, owned a produce store at 4508 Liberty Avenue and resided on Dargan Street.

This beautiful couple, Giacinda Donatelli and Luigi Rainaldi, married on January 20, 1896. Of their 13 children, 8 survived: 5 well-known brothers and their 3 sisters, many of whom owned businesses in Bloomfield. Giacinda and Luigi lived at 4610 Carroll Street until their passing.

In 1936, Leonzio Carlini, stonecutter for Campbell-Horgan Monument Company, is shown chiseling a Frank Vittor design onto the Westinghouse Bridge. Carlini and his wife, Teresa, from San Pietro, Avellano, Italy, resided on Cedarville Street with daughters Frances, Roseanna, and Norma. Frances Carlini Gasbarro continues to reside there.

The Pearl Street Meat Market at 210 Pearl Street was built by Joseph J. Reder Sr. in 1931. His son, Joseph Jr., worked in the market from age 16 and purchased it from the family after his father's passing in 1950. The Pearl Street Meat Market closed in 1985; however, the family still resides in the dwelling.

Dominic Covelli owned and operated the Bloomfield Fruit Market at 4953 Liberty Avenue. He worked seven days a week and did not close his store until 11:00 p.m. His children, Lucille and Joseph, worked in the family business until Dominic Covelli's passing in 1971. Joseph continued on as a strong community advocate on the Bloomfield Citizens Council Board of Directors and was honored with the Outstanding Citizen Award in 2002.

The C. J. Hoffman family business name has graced their location at 4716 Liberty Avenue in the 19th, 20th, and 21st centuries from 1892 until the present. It is Bloomfield's oldest business, multigenerational owned. In this picture from the 1960s are, from left to right, Urban, James, William, and Christian. The family was active in St. Joseph Parish and played a visible role sponsoring community events, children's programs, and athletics.

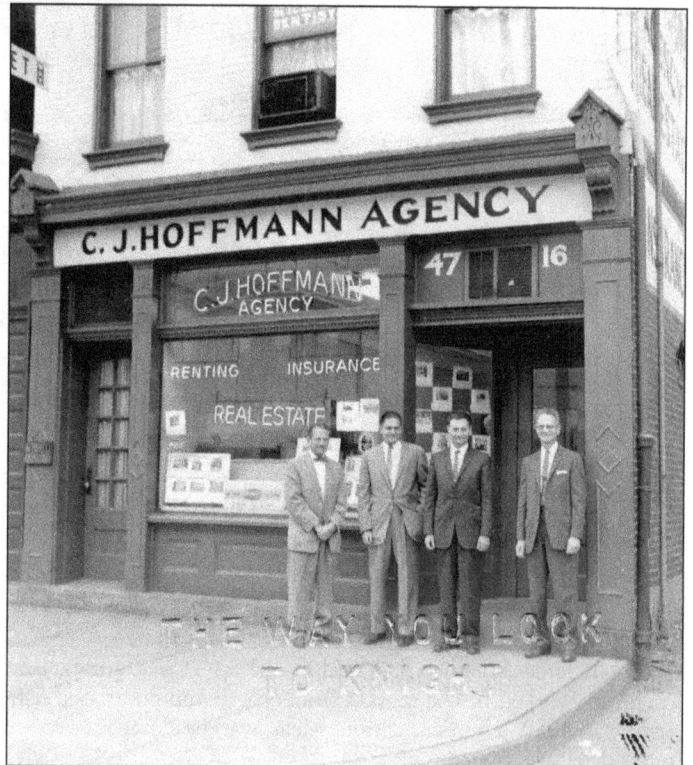

Walter Lendl of the Lendl Bakery family at 4516 Liberty Avenue was also a baker at St. Francis Hospital. Walter is seen stacking hot loaves right out of the oven. Every day, 250 loaves of bread were baked in the hospital kitchen along with rolls, buns, and cakes to feed 1,100 patients three times a day.

Mascio Tailors Men's Wear and Dry Cleaning Store was opened by John Mascio in 1936 and was family run for 54 years. In the 1900s, men's suits cost $22 and Mascio had a Suit Club for $2 weekly for 11 weeks to save for a suit with two pairs of trousers. John and his wife, Marguerite Sciullo, were both from Abruzzo, Italy, and met and married in Bloomfield.

Sr. Mary Concetta Gentile lived on Edmond Street with her parents Dominic and Vincentia Ranallo Gentile and five siblings. Upon entering the order of the Pallottine Missionary Sisters, she was assigned to teach at Immaculate Conception School in the 1940s.

In 1941, this eight-room brick school was dedicated and the priests moved into the new rectory on Friendship Avenue during Fr. Florinda DeFrancesco's tenure. In 1953, Fr. Albert Farina added five additional rooms and a 12-room convent at the corner of Friendship Avenue and Edmond Street. The Pallotine Sisters left and the Sisters of the Holy Spirit came and continue to teach into the 21st century.

Henry Edwardo was an altar boy at Immaculate Conception Church, shown in the background. Throughout his grade-school years, he took accordion lessons from Frank Salpietro, who taught music in between haircuts at his barbershop on Cedarville Street. Edwardo continues to play music professionally and is among four generations of his family still living in Bloomfield.

In 1948, the graduating class from Immaculate Conception School had its picture taken by beloved local photographer Alfred Cardell, and as true to one style, three priests are seated in the front row with the shortest girls in the class standing and the tallest boys in the top row and at each end. Occasionally, the nuns got to have a different position, that being top left, right, or center. Pictured standing at the center of the second row from the top is Principal Sister Amelia, and seated in front, from left to right, are Fr. William Frawley, Fr. Florindo DeFrancesco, and Fr. Dominic Olivieri.

Realtor and photographer William Kovach worked and lived in the neighborhood operating at the Berkshire Realty, located at 4748 Liberty Avenue between Isaly's Ice Cream Store and North American Business Machines Corporation. Liberty Avenue's business district has always been very diversified.

These 22 gorgeous Bloomfield girls (and they were girls in those days) are celebrating a victorious bowling tournament at J. L. Thomas Bar, 4648 Liberty Avenue. Mrs. Thomas is seated third from the left wearing a corsage. She must have been one of the team captains. They bowled duck pins in the alleys downstairs of Spaniards (later Peerless Department Store and now Citizens Bank) on the corner of Liberty Avenue and Pearl Street.

This photograph of Mary Bianco and son Frank Bianco Jr., taken in the 1940s, represents the patriotic spirit of the day when it was very popular for young boys to wear a sailor cap retrieved from some relative and have friends autograph it. Note how well dressed Mary is while taking her son to Kennywood Amusement Park.

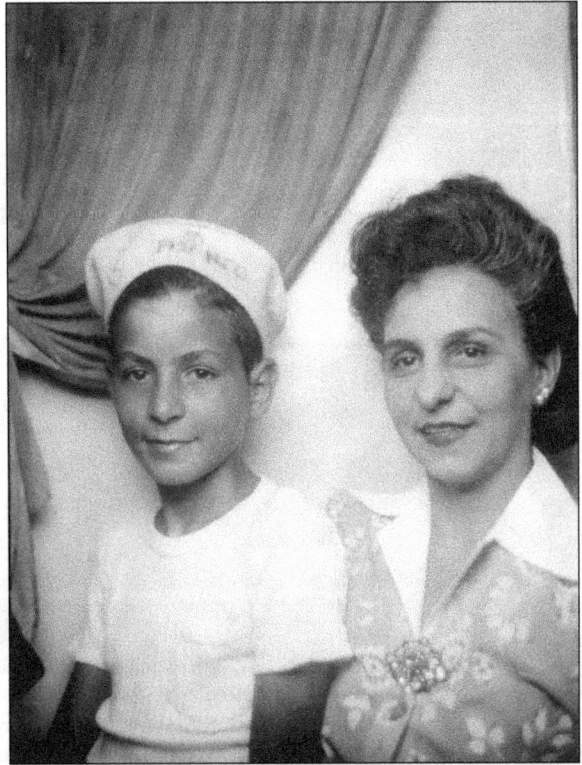

Camaraderie and patriotism were in abundance during World War II at the J. L. Thomas Bar, 4502 Liberty Avenue. Thomas himself (shown in the right foreground) hung the dismantled bomb from the ceiling (above left) and kept an honor roll wall adorned with pictures of servicemen so that they would not be forgotten by the people back home.

The women of Bloomfield had close friendships, and bowling was a great sport for a night out. The women's bowling league used alleys downstairs of Ralph Spaniard's department store at the corner of Pearl Street and Liberty Avenue. Citizens Bank is now in that location.

Albert Edwardo, a first-generation American with nine siblings, loved the Italian customs until his passing in 2007. Here he is shown leading the St. Rocco/Blessed Mother parade on Lorigan Street. The bands played for three days with the promise of Italian meals and wine. The Edwardo family cooked and opened up their home on Juniper Street to make the event happen for Bloomfield.

CASTEL
DI
SANGRO

This photograph is of Castel Di Sangro, a town in Abruzzo, Italy. A very large segment of the population settled in Bloomfield and even came on the same steamship ocean liner together. A club was located on Cedarville Street and was really constructed from a party-wall house sitting on a deep lot. A bar meeting room and bocce courts made it a social haven for the Italians of Bloomfield.

The Italian Ladies Bocce League met at the Castel Di Sangro Club on Cedarville Street for games and competition for decades starting in the 1940s. Almost all of the women are related to each other as sisters or cousins. The gentleman in the center is Alex Alviani. At least a dozen of the women are his sisters, sisters-in-law, and first cousins. Alviani was president of the Castel Di Sangro Club.

One Sunday afternoon in the early days of 1924, several Ateleta men gathered at the Bloomfield Italian Independent Club on Lorigan Street to plan their own fraternal organization. Their first elected president was Cecidio Ricci. Emil Lucente was their longest-presiding president. Men are shown in coveralls two decades later preparing to build their own club.

There was always a reason to celebrate among the Zappa family members and friends. A backyard beer party on Taylor Street in 1938 was fine with Papa Zappa looking on from the rear. What better reason to get 13 men together?

The Bloomfield Italian Independent Club on Lorigan Street was one of the first fraternal organizations to form within the immigration movement. The Lorigan Street area also had 22 businesses, one of them being the Iacovetti Bank at the corner of Lorigan and Edmond Streets. Proud members attend a Sunday picnic dressed in white shirts, ties, and straw hats.

William "Sherlock" Sciullo is surrounded by friends on a Sunday afternoon at the Bloomfield Italian Independent Club on Lorigan Street. Lifelong friendships had grown from those casual get-togethers. Seated from left to right are Papa Carnevale, Andrew Pietrone, Sherlock, and Ernest Carnevale. Standing are "Piney" Disipio, "Barrone," Peter Orsini, Al DiBucci, Al Carnevale, and Daniel DeShantz.

Francesco Donatelli, born in Ateleta, Italy, was simply warm hearted and loving to his granddaughter Patti Jean Donatelli, daughter of Dominic and Helen Donatelli. She showed as much love in return and was always fascinated that her dog, Skippy, understood when her "Tuddone" spoke to him in Italian. Neither one could do any wrong in the other's eyes, as is evidenced in this beautiful photograph. The family resided together on Edmond Street.

Albert Edwardo (left) is shown with his father Amerigo (center) and *compare* Meraldo Bertoni Sr. (right) on a Sunday visit. Amerigo came from Roccacinquemiglia, Italy, and raised 10 children with his wife, Genuina. Note how popular pin-striped suits were in the 1940s, and of course the fedora hat from Emil Everdard's Mens Store at Liberty Avenue and Pearl Street.

Brotherly love is shown on a family outing for the sons of Luigi Rainaldi. From left to right are (first row) Anthony and Edward; (second row) Enrico, Albert, and Joseph. Albert worked as a butcher and grocery store owner on Torley Street. Enrico, Anthony, and Edward were painters for Warner Brothers Theaters. Rainaldi Interiors store was at the corner of Penn Avenue and Main Street, formerly the all-night eatery the Regal Restaurant.

This picture is of the Jene-Mager Post 278 on 4660 Gangwish Street after World War II. Note that the first veteran on the left in the front row is wearing the Purple Heart medal that signifies he was wounded in combat. The veterans' organization received its charter on November 16, 1919.

Herman Lendl transferred to the tank division in World War II. He was first reported missing in action and then officially reported killed in action on January 2, 1945. His sister, Helen Lendl Nothwang, still resides in Bloomfield.

Pvt. George J. Visconti died on September 12, 1944, in a military hospital in England from wounds sustained during the Invasion of Normandy. Visconti resided at 456 Pearl Street. His sister, Delores Visconti Fantone, still resides in Bloomfield.

Pfc. William N. Spiri died on June 22, 1944, at Normandy, France. He resided at 227 Edmond Street. His sisters, Catherine and Dorothy, still reside in Bloomfield.

James W. Madden served in the armed forces and was killed in the Battle of the Bulge in Belgium on February 9, 1944. He resided at 441 Ella Street. His daughter-in-law, Viola Mosco Madden, and her children remain Bloomfield residents on Cedarville Street.

S.Sgt. Nicholas DelCimmuto was a ball turret gunner aboard a bomber. He resided at 3950 Liberty Avenue. He died after his 25th mission over occupied Europe on March 15, 1944. This photograph was taken with his neighbor Rose Carcione when he was home on his last leave.

For Easter in 1943, Lawrence, 101st Airborne; Frank "Cabbie," U.S. Navy; and Dominic, 101st Airborne, surprised their parents Dominic and Vincenzia Ranallo Gentile with a military leave visit. Their other brother, Albert, is not shown. Lawrence and Dominic, twins, asked to stay together and were on the same raid in Holland. Dominic was shot and killed during the air drop.

Pfc. Cornelius Obermeier
Field Artillery
Son of
Mrs. Anna Obermeier,
4605 Carroll Street

Cyril Obermeier, S 2/c
Naval Air Base
Son of
Mrs. Anna Obermeier,
4605 Carroll Street

Pvt. Herbert Obermeier
Medical Detachment
Son of
Mrs. Anna Obermeier,
4605 Carroll Street

John Schimmel, F 1/c
Navy
Husband of
Mrs. John Schimmel,
517 Osceola Street

The four men pictured are three Obermeier brothers and brother-in-law John Schimmel serving in World War II at the same time. Another brother, Cornelius, served in the armed forces during this time but is not pictured here. Anna Obermeier was the mother of the three men and mother-in-law of Schimmel. She worked on fund drives for the Community Chest (now United Way), even though she was left a young widow with seven children in 1939.

U.S. Navy sailor William Bradley served from 1943 to 1946 and received ribbons for the European theater and the Pacific theater. He served on the USS *Nevada* and resided on Carroll Street until his passing.

Sgt. Jack Sciullo served in the armed forces from 1941 to 1945. He was wounded on Anzio Beach in Italy, and received the Purple Heart. He returned home from the service on December 13, 1945, and resided at 421 Pearl Street.

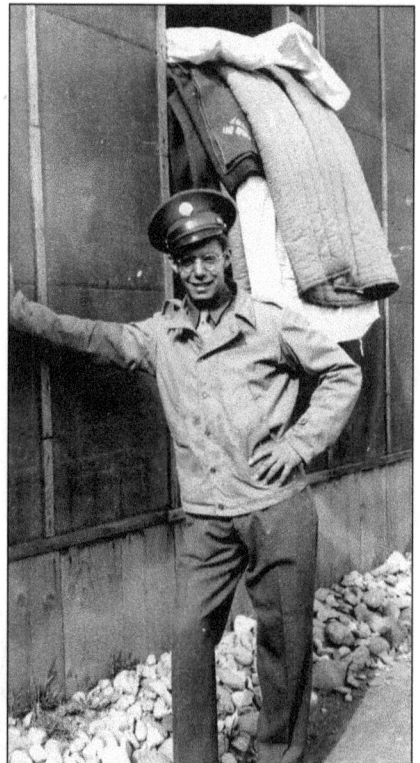

Pvt. Anthony Sciullo served in the U.S. Army from 1942 to 1944. He was stationed in London and loaded bombers with live bombs for missions. He resided at 451 Cedarville Street.

Pvt. Pietro Fantone, 133rd Infantry Regiment of the 34th Infantry Division from 1943 to 1945, was wounded on January 5, 1944, in Italy. He was awarded the Purple Heart, Good Conduct Medal, and the European-African-Middle Eastern Service Medal with four bronze stars.

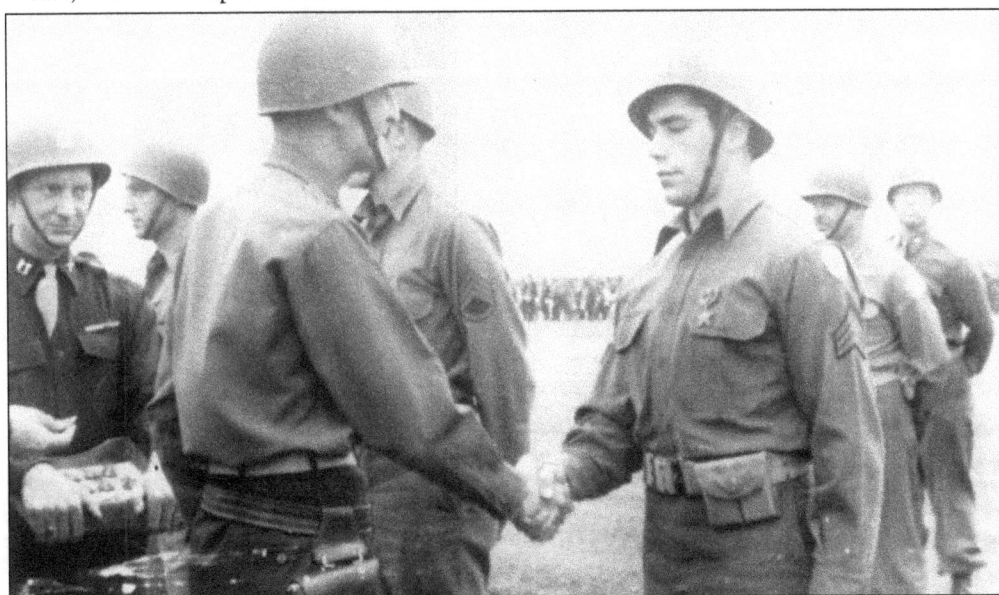

Anthony Donatelli, sergeant in the Coast Artillery Corps Headquarters Battery A, 480th Anti-Aircraft Artillery Automatic Weapons Batallion (semi-mobile), U.S. Army, received the Bronze Star Medal from Gen. Curtis Lemay for meritorious service in connection with military operations from 1944 to 1945. He also received the European-African-Middle Eastern Campaign Medal, World War II Victory Medal, American Campaign Medal, and Good Conduct Medal. In September 2008, Donatelli was the recipient of the Bloomfield Citizens Council Patriotism Award.

Joseph Vanucci struts with pride next to son Richard walking on Cedarville Street during a military leave. Richard enlisted from 1940 to 1945 and was a U.S. Air Force mechanic. He achieved the rank of sergeant.

Peter Mascio is shown home on leave with his parents Marguerite and John Mascio. John Mascio, a clothier and tailor, was always impeccably dressed with a tailored three-piece suit and fedora hat. Peter was the recipient of a Purple Heart.

Sailor Frank Carcione is shown with his mother, Angelina Fazio Carcione, and father, Samuel, on leave at their 4012 Liberty Avenue home. Frank served from 1946 to 1948. His parents were both immigrants from Sicily, Italy. Note Pittsburgh Erie Saw in the background.

There is nothing like a football game back home with friends and neighbors. Seated from left to right are August Carlino, Anna Marie Mariani, Edward Mariani, Reynolds Caruso, and a friend home on leave from the navy. The man shown in the fedora, standing on the far right, is John "Brother" Walters.

The plan to erect a World War II monument in Morrow Park, gateway to Bloomfield, was instituted by Samuel Juliano, owner of the Little Cottage restaurant at 4624 Liberty Avenue. The well-known Pittsburgh sculptor Frank Vittor erected an 18-foot-high limestone memorial sculpted on three sides with a sailor, airman, and a soldier. When funding fell short, Juliano and his wife Adeline provided $5,300 that they never recovered. He died on February 25, 1948, 16 months before the unveiling. Adeline was part of the ceremony and dedication on June 14, 1949. Earlier in 1922, the park had been named for Eustes Morrow who was the longest Pittsburgh city controller, in office for almost 40 years, and lived across the street on Liberty Avenue.

George Caloger, U.S. Navy, posed in uniform at the request of famous sculptor Frank Vittor in 1944 for his sculpting of the sailor on the World War II Bloomfield monument. Vittor was meticulous in his efforts to put the 13 stars on Caloger's belt and the silk scarf he referred to as the "tie." This came by personal request from Little Cottage owner Samuel Juliano.

Richard Renckly, armed forces, posed in uniform at the request of famous sculptor Frank Vittor in 1944 for his sculpting of the soldier on the World War II Bloomfield monument. Vittor was described as portly, distinguished, and easy to get along with. The event was a personal request from Edward Staudt, president of Pioneer Savings and Loan Bank.

The monument behind friends Ann Collinger (left), Mariana Lombardo (center), and Ann LeDonne seemingly vanished from Friendship Park around the 1950s. The bronze artifact that circled a flagpole was never recovered, despite the combined efforts of city officials and the Bloomfield Citizens Council.

West Penn Hospital came to Bloomfield in 1912, located on the Winebiddle Woods. Friendship Park served as the hospital front at this original entrance and the emergency room entrance was to the left. The school of nursing was completed in 1923 and today is the only hospital-based school in Pittsburgh. Major expansion took place though the 1960s and the 1980s with construction of Mellon Pavilion, a heliport, laundry, and new towers.

Receiving the sacrament of communion is a sacred religious and family event for the Pannunzio-Buzzelli family. Father Joseph, mother Concetta, and grandmother Theresa Talotta Buzzelli (second row) honor Larry, wearing communion suit, as brother Lenny and aunt Flo give special attention. The single-story building in the background is Samson Buick at the corner of Liberty and Pacific Avenues.

Mayor David L. Lawrence is shown dancing with Mary Cercone at the Bloomfield Civics 1946 championship banquet where he gave the keynote address. Lawrence lived in Bloomfield, raising his family at 355 South Aiken Avenue. Lawrence served as mayor from 1946 to 1959 and won the election for governor of Pennsylvania in 1958, becoming the only Pittsburgh mayor to do so. Bloomfield is the only Pittsburgh neighborhood that can boast of having a mayor and a governor in residence. He maintained his home and contact with the people of Bloomfield until he died on November 21, 1966.

"Jumpin' Joe" Barone is shown in a 1946 photograph in the air during a Golden Glove title championship fight that he won in New York. He turned professional after that victory. Jumpin' Joe was known for jumping up to reach his opponents that were usually much taller than him. He was trained professionally by the well-known Ralph Martzo.

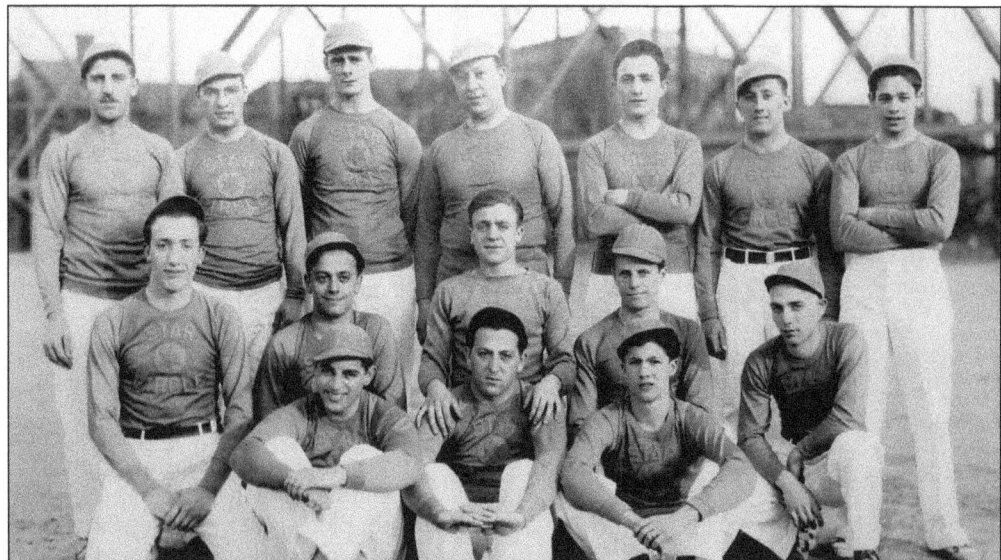

The Star Circle Mushball team, now called softball, was comprised of young Bloomfield men from Immaculate Conception Parish. They were in the Holy Name Lyceum together and contributed volunteer time to the church as ushers and assistants and continued to do so as senior citizens. It became a way of life for many of them.

Anthony "Red" Celender's family consisted of 10 brothers and sisters with hardworking parents from Calabria, Italy. Red played 200 football games for Dan Cercone's Bloomfield Civics and mostly for Charles Rogers's Bloomfield Rams. His position was either half-back or linebacker. In the 1955 Steel Bowl Championship game, Red scored twice on handoffs from Johnny Unitas. Red was Bloomfield's finest football player of modern times—the "Steelman of Sandlot."

After 10 games that season, the Civics were 8-1-1 and in first place. The Pittsburgh sports writers had taken notice and began writing stories in all the papers. The 1946 Civics football team was the toast of Bloomfield. The Civics had to play the game without fullback Charles Fahl, who was injured in a previous game. Nunzio Galioto switched to fullback position and scored the game's only touchdown. The Civics were the champions.

William Reynolds, motor machinist first class, U.S. Navy, was a past commander of the VFW Post 278 for two separate terms. He is one of the leading military historians in the United States and spanned 70 years of public service in veterans' affairs. Most notably, Reynolds places over 1,000 flags on veterans' graves for Memorial Day annually and on 400 Civil War graves.

Raymond Fern, sergeant, U.S. Air Force 1951–1953, served in Korea from 1952 to 1953. Past commander of the VFW Post 278 for three terms, District 29 commander of the VFW, and the only Pittsburgher to be elected as international supreme commander of the Military Order of the Cootie (honor degree of the VFW), Raymond is a past recipient of the Bloomfield Citizens Council Patriotism Award.

Five

THE FABULOUS
1950s AND 1960s

Serviceman were coming and going again with another war—this time it was Korea. Nevertheless, love was in the air. The high school crowd traded in their saddle shoes for loafers and the ballads of the 1940s for rock and roll.

Gone were the bicycles, skates, and gigs (homemade wooden scooters). This generation had grown up quickly and were the proud owners of second-hand and third-hand cars. Every corner drugstore and tavern would continue to be the special place where groups of friends would develop lifelong relationships. Sports would continue to be alive and well.

The second wave of Italian immigration was in full swing and brought stunning changes. The hardworking, hard-saving families achieved their American dream—owning a home. Jobs paralleled ownership as *pisanos* would help each other, providing labor to remodel their homes. Immaculate Conception Parish would build the present-day church.

The three local hospitals, West Penn, St. Francis, and Shadyside, were fast expanding their physical plants and schools of nursing. The Italian immigrants were embraced by the hospitals as employees because of their strong work ethic. Friends recommended friends as more of the wives joined the hospital workforce. In some households fathers, mothers, sons, and daughters would all be employed outside the home.

Anything was possible in America; everything was possible in Bloomfield.

Massimo Delledonne arrived in America from Abruzzo, Italy, in 1912. He returned to Italy and married Sabatina and they had one daughter, Gloria. Because of the wars, quotas set by the government, and a lack of money, the immigrants worked to save for boat passage. Sabatina arrived in America in 1947, Gloria in 1955, and her husband, Nicola Balestra, came with their two daughters in 1956.

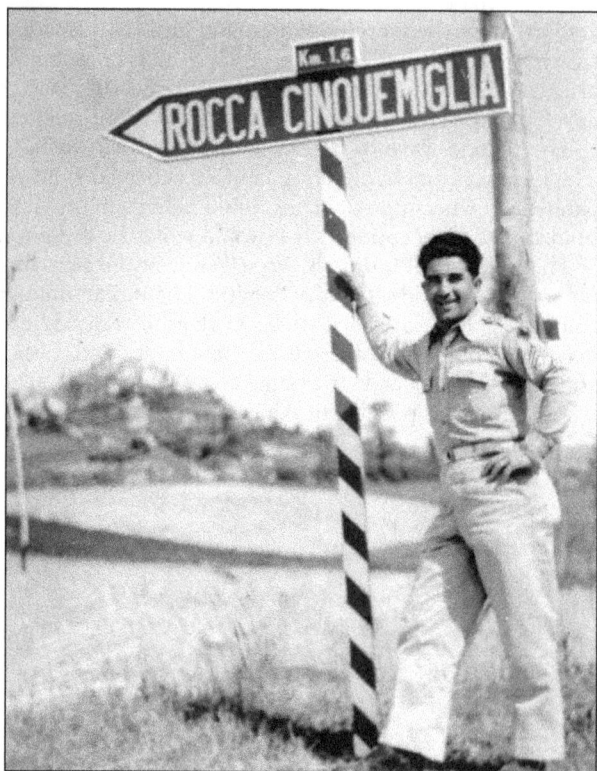

Victor Santucci came to America from Roccacinquemiglia, Abruzzo, Italy, as a young adult. He later enlisted in the armed forces and did a tour of duty in Europe, returning to see his hometown. After discharge, he continued to reside in Bloomfield and met and married Ida DelSignore, also from Abruzzo, Italy. Victor owned Vic's Little Cottage Restaurant at 4624 Liberty Avenue, which is now Gator's Pub.

A reflection of inner beauty is displayed on the face of Genuina Lecce Eduardo, dressed with jewelry and white stockings and holding flowers. She immigrated originally from Roccacinquemiglia, Abruzzo, Italy. She and her husband, Amerigo Eduardo, had 10 children and resided at 474 Juniper Street until her passing in 1983.

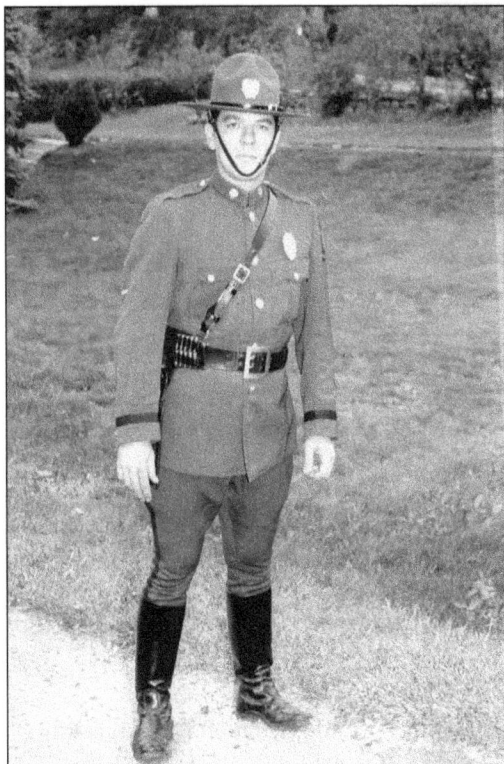

The Allegheny County policeman is Elmo Buzzelli, whose colorful job (to ride a horse for a living) fascinated his boyhood friends. Buzzelli began working for Allegheny County Police Department in 1959 and retired in 1982 after a serious spill from a motorcycle (the horse was safer).

The Immaculate Conception Parish traditionally had a procession in Friendship Park of the Girls Sodality on the first of May to crown a statue of the Blessed Mother with flowers. Pictured in their backyard are Sodality sisters and onetime May Queens Dolores Damico (1951), Rose DeAngelis, and Gloria Kalench (1950).

It was a joyous occasion when John Damico Jr. was home on leave from the armed forces. Pictured are his father, John Sr., his brother Edward, and youngest sister Phyllis. The two decorative stars in front of their home were part of the construction. A third-generation Damico is still residing there at 411 Ella Street.

Lt. Col. (retired) Margaret A. Gentile, BSN, one of six children of Domenic and Vincentie Ranallo Gentile of Edmond Street, began her nursing career at St. Francis Hospital. She entered the U.S. Air Force Nurse Corps in January 1964 following 10 years of general practice and earned the Defense Ribbon, Longevity Ribbon, Air Force Commendation Medal with oak leaf cluster, and the Service Medal with three oak leaf clusters.

A trip back to the Statue of Liberty in New York in June 1952 awakened memories for Emil Lucente, who came to America from Ateleta, Abruzzo, Italy, in 1929 on the steamship *Roma*. Lucente and his wife, Almerinda, provided the experience for children Edward, twins Elizabeth and Virginia, and Angelo, who were very impressed.

Kate's Dairy Store at 4613 Liberty Avenue, with jukebox blaring inside with Rosemary Clooney's "Come ona My House," was the scene of this Sunday afternoon photograph during the Korean War era. From left to right, in uniform, Felix Mannella and Ralph McCall are standing next to Sam Juliano Jr. (civilian) and Peter Orr, who was out of his 28th Division guard uniform.

From left to right, lifelong buddies Russell Carlisle, Edward Autenbaugh, and Jerry Hammill pose in front of the W. D. Larkin Plumbing and Heating Store at 4611 Liberty Avenue next door to Kate's Dairy Store in the Korean War era. Somehow they always managed to get leave on the weekends to see the Bloomfield girls. They were all grass roots buddies who came back to their hometown after the service and started married life in Bloomfield.

Fred Mackaness not only worked in Mierzwa's Drug Store at 4724 Liberty Avenue as a fountain boy growing up, but he also worked in Aiello Drug Store and Isaly's making skyscraper ice-cream cones. His sister Eileen worked at Bloomfield Drug Store, sister Maureen worked at Carroll's Drug Store, and brothers Howard and William also worked at Mierzwa's Drug Store. They were very active in St. Joseph Parish.

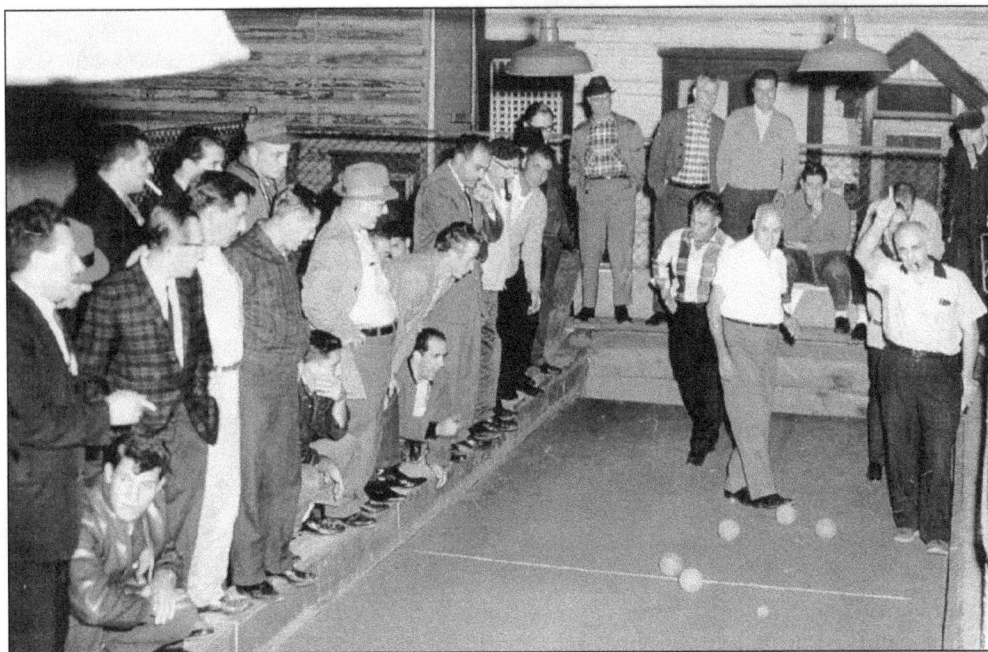

The Dan Cercone bocce team plays bocce at the Castel Di Sangro courts in 1940 with Michael Tramonte calling score. The tournaments were a regular component of holiday gatherings and Italian religious festivals. These games, at times, resulted in heated demonstrations of bowling skills.

John Unitas played for $6 a game for coach Charles Rogers and the Bloomfield Rams of the Greater Pittsburgh League at Dean's and Arsenal Fields. The Steelers told Unitas they had too many quarterbacks. While playing for Bloomfield he tried out for the Baltimore Colts. They signed him for $7,000 in 1956 and he began a 17-year-career as their quarterback.

The confidence in Unitas's steely gaze quickly marked him as the leader the Colts had been waiting for.

No-nonsense coach Charles "Bear" Rogers and coach Ben Di Cola have the attention of the Bloomfield Italian Independent Club players. Bear received his nickname from one of his protégés, Anthony "Red" Celender. He coached sandlot with John Unitas, paid the guys $6 a game, and then fined them $3 for cussing during practice. Bear was athletic director at Immaculate Conception for 28 years. Bloomfield is providing a record of his achievements, that can be seen at the John Heinz History Center.

The Bloomfield Trojans were a rugged team from the 1950s. They started out as teams with street names, such as Ella, Lorigan, Taylor, Carroll, and many others that played on Saturday morning on Dean's dirt, stony field. No pads or pants and clod hoppers were a common sight. They just loved sandlot football.

The 1955 Bloomfield Bears went undefeated 10-0. The team was coached by Louis LeDonne and played neighboring communities. The team sold boosters to pay for their uniforms. Every two years, since 1955, they continue to have reunions sustaining the close friendships formed in their early years of growing up in Bloomfield.

Pictured is the Immaculate Conception altar in 1950. Fr. Domenic Oliveri is officiating at the Evelyn Carlini and Paul Costa wedding. One of the angels mounted on the left and right arch made in 1910 was going to be discarded after being stored in the basement of the Plaza Theater. A longtime parishioner rescued the statue and stored it in her home for safekeeping. She offered it to Fr. John Dinello, had it restored, and it now sits in the lobby of Immaculate Conception Church dedicated to deceased children. Its appraised value is $28,000.

The Immaculate Conception Catholic School first grade class of 1966 follows a tradition of escorting the First Holly Communion class to the altar as "little angels." Shown from left to right are Darlene Allan, Anna Marie Scullion, Nina Mariani, Carol Long, Diane Mastriani, Maureen Weimerskirch, Lisa Peluso, and Joanne Bucci. A group photograph would be taken later in Friendship Park by photographer Alfred Cardell.

On October 23, 1960, the cornerstone was blessed by Monsignor Henry Carlin. Pastor Rev. Albert Farina would begin a massive economic development project by purchasing all of the homes on Edmond and Cedarville Streets in hopes of expanding the school and church during his tenure from March 1951 to January 1969. Plans changed, and the property was sold to the City of Pittsburgh for a metered parking lot to be shared by the parish during special events.

Born Catherine Eleanor Milligan in Fairmont, West Virginia, on March 29, 1888, Mother DeChantel passed away in 1997 at an Ursuline Sister facility in Louisville, Kentucky. She was 109 years old. She was the principal at Ursuline Academy private grade school and high school located at 201 Winebiddle Street throughout most of the 20th century. Today that building is Waldorf grade school.

Pharmacist Bernard Danenberg holds a sign saying "this one is Hank Stohl" behind the children's television star during a special guest appearance as an elated Phyllis Danenberg looks on. The husband and wife team often held special events at their Bloomfield Drug Store on the corner of Liberty Avenue and Cedarville Street making the neighborhood extra special for children.

Andrews School was torn down and a beautiful neighborhood swimming pool was built on Ella Street. It is still being used. Jumping off a diving board was a major thrill for youngsters. Parents would stand at the cyclone fence to keep an eye on their children. The building in the background is Mission Hall, a popular social hall for weddings and parties before it was razed.

Six

A Step Back in Time

Bloomfield was standing strong against urban decay and huge population shifts in Pittsburgh during the 1970s and 1980s.

It was a community of employed people, husbands, wives, and children alike that kept the economy strong and the avenue bustling. The general atmosphere was quaint and refreshing. It was charming to hear a second language spoken in the stores and on the streets. To observe the old European custom of widows dressed in black going to church, shopping, and sweeping their sidewalks was another throwback in time.

The sound of church bells resounding at the Angelus times, 6:00 a.m., 12:00 noon, and 6:00 p.m., was a unique Catholic custom that still continues into the 21st century.

Family and friends were always nearby to share laughter and tears through significant events from cradle to grave. The custom from the old country, of making wine, was never lost in Bloomfield.

Yet in direct dichotomy to the old-fashioned village characteristics, modern-day politics would raise the excitement and tempers within political campaigns. The scarcity of registered Republicans left the Democrats the colorful opportunity to have strong differences of opinion within their own party.

Election time was always a time of civil unrest in Bloomfield.

The basketball team was named the Yankees because Joseph Lupone (second row, left) loved Joseph DiMaggio and the New York Yankees. He is joined by, from left to right, (first row) John Pelusi, Sal Visconti, and Paul "Max" Sciullo; (second row) Steve Peters. They routinely practiced every Saturday morning and some evenings at the Bloomfield Recreation Center for five years.

TOPS was the acronym for Take off Pounds Sensibly and started in Bloomfield by the late Blanche Chessey in 1970 as Chapter 559. The friendships that developed were also a positive outcome for the popular group that met at the United Methodist Church on Mathilda Street across from the Liedertafel club.

Pictured, from left to right, are three generations of the Norma Donatelli Fiegel family spending time with hometown friends during a marathon festival. Cousins Wendy and Chelsea share the stroller as Norma "Gram," daughter Pam Ranallo, and daughter-in-law Kathy Fiegel walk the avenue. This photograph represents the charm of villagelike Bloomfield.

Joseph Wehrheim continued to use his artistic talents to create floral arrangements at the Wehrheim Floral Shop, located at 4709 Liberty Avenue, long after his father, George, had started it in 1908. Joseph was born inside the house in back of the business. He served on every possible committee at St. Joseph Church and was a VFW Post 278 commander. He always had his dog, Shag, at the floral shop.

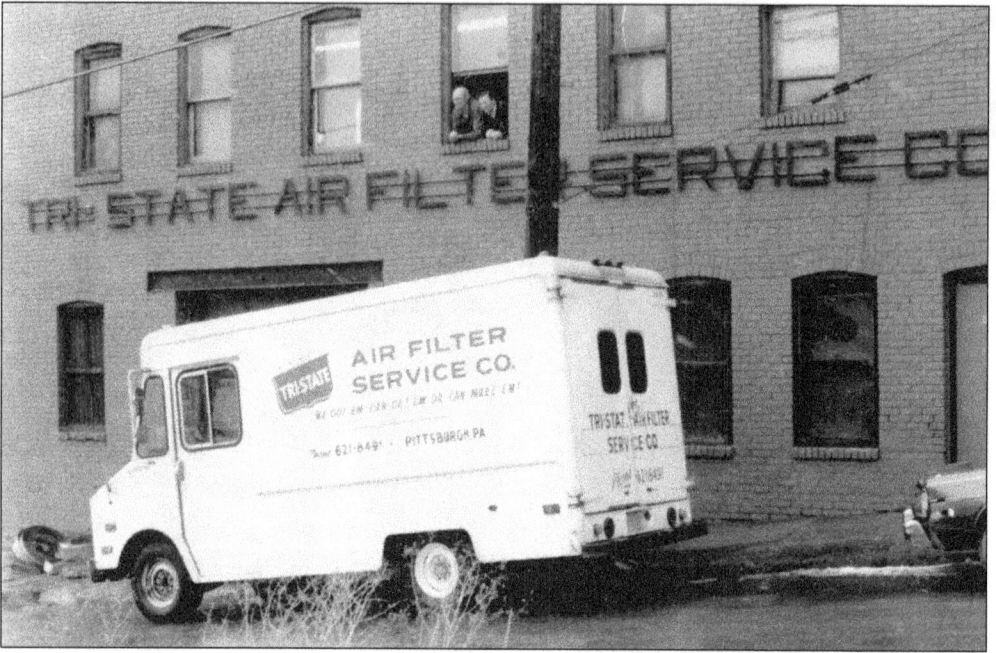

TriState Filter Company is a business that makes special to-order heating and air conditioning filters for commercial and residential customers. Since 1926, the building at 744 Edmond Street at the corner of Juniper Street has been used for that purpose. Robert and Gloria LeDonne, who reside across the street, have owned it since 1987.

The sacrament of confirmation at Immaculate Conception Church was given to John Damico (left), Robert Buzzelli (center), and Daniel Scullion (right) in 1977. Leisure suits, long hair, and large ties were the rage. The boys all went on to graduate Central Catholic High School where Daniel Scullion played football as defensive tackle when Dan Marino was team captain, and Scullion went on to captain the team in 1980. Damico is a fireman and resides in Australia, Buzzelli is vice president of Fifth Third Bank, and Scullion is a regional sales representative for Simpson Strongtie in North Carolina.

In April 1984, Mayor Richard Caliguiri honored Dan and Mary Damico Cercone with the key to the city for their role in Pittsburgh as community leaders, mentors, benefactors, role models, and friends to all. This honor is usually reserved for international people. Dan and Mary, a gifted husband-and-wife team, made a profound difference in the lives of others.

Friends and relatives attended the key to the city of Pittsburgh award ceremony in April 1984 for Dan and Mary Cercone (standing, center) with Mayor Richard Caliguiri. The couple provided financial assistance and the sponsorship needed to come to America and leave war-torn Italy after the quotas were lifted for Italians. This was seen as a great humanitarian gesture.

Impact, derailment, toxic spill, and fire were four events that occurred almost simultaneously under the Bloomfield Bridge. At 12:35 p.m. on April 11, 1987, a boxcar carrying thousands of phonograph record burnings was spewing toxic chemicals throughout Bloomfield, causing the entire community to be evacuated.

The Bloomfield Citizens Council hosted congressional hearings for Sen. John Heinz at the Immaculate Conception hall following the derailment and toxic spill on April 11, 1987. Senator Heinz blasted the Federal Railroad Administration for under staffing the Pittsburgh office. This photograph was taken at the derailment site. Shown here, from left to right, are Martin Foley, U.S. senator John Heinz, Bob Scullion Sr., Janet Scullion, Patty Ladasky, and John Steinbaugh.

The Clyde Kelly, Branch 84, Letter Carriers Band is the official music arm of the Pittsburgh Letter Carriers Association. The band practiced regularly at the Bloomfield Liedertafel Singing Society Club. Marching in the foreground, playing the saxophone, is John "Bud" Kennel. The late Bennie DiCola and Anthony Mianzo were also band members.

The Welcome to Bloomfield wall was donated to the community at a cost of $9,000 by Patrick Media at the request of the Bloomfield Citizens Council in 1988. That year, the advocacy group sold white T-shirts with letters that spelled Bloomfield in individual flowerpots. They quickly became a collector's item.

Robert Scullion Sr. of the Bloomfield Citizens Council Board of Directors playfully holds cardboard scissors used to cut the ribbon on Bloomfield's new bridge in November 1986. His two sons, John (left) and Joseph (right), and his older brother Jack join the fun. The first bridge opened on November 19, 1914, and was torn down in 1980. It took six years to get the new one completed.

Mayor Richard Caliguiri along with pastor Fr. Domenic Oliveri, Pastor John Janzura of Immaculate Heart of Mary Church, and councilmen Jack Wagner and Richard Givens rode the Iron City Beer Wagon across the new Bloomfield Bridge on November 1, 1986. Five-thousand spectators came to the Bloomfield Citizens Council public event.

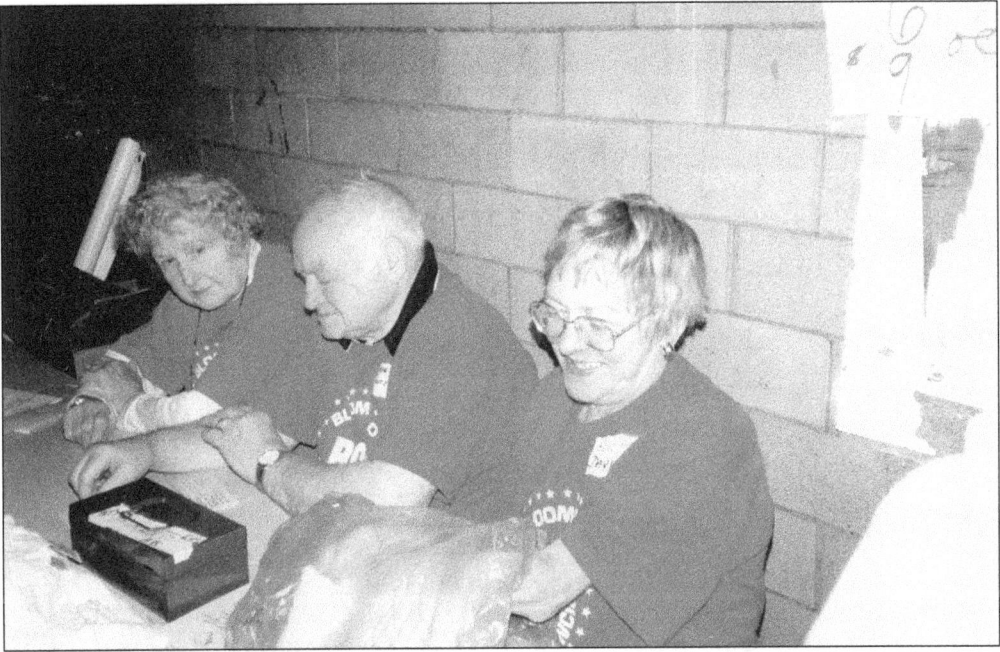

Bloomfield Citizens Council members Peggy Davis, Victor Infante, and Ruth Infante sell T-shirts as a fund-raiser in the Immaculate Conception gymnasium. Members of the community were honored for special achievements. The friendships formed through public service were genuine and lasted a lifetime.

Musician Robert Scullion Jr. and the Mystics Rock and Roll Band have been a fixture at Bloomfield at events since they organized in 1969 while attending Central Catholic High School. This picture was taken during the Pittsburgh Marathon under the canopy of the Plaza Theater. In 2009, the group will celebrate its 40th anniversary together. Seen here are, from left to right, Mark Coch on guitar, Bob Scullion on vibes, Paul Toma and Ron Donatucci on guitars, and Nick Dialuso on saxophone.

Maj. Richard Givens retired from the U.S. Air Force after 20 years of service, 250 combat missions, and the decorations to prove it. He came back with his politically astute wife, Ethel Coleman Givens, and their eight children. The entire family won the hearts of Pittsburghers when he ran for Pittsburgh City Council and served for 16 consecutive years.

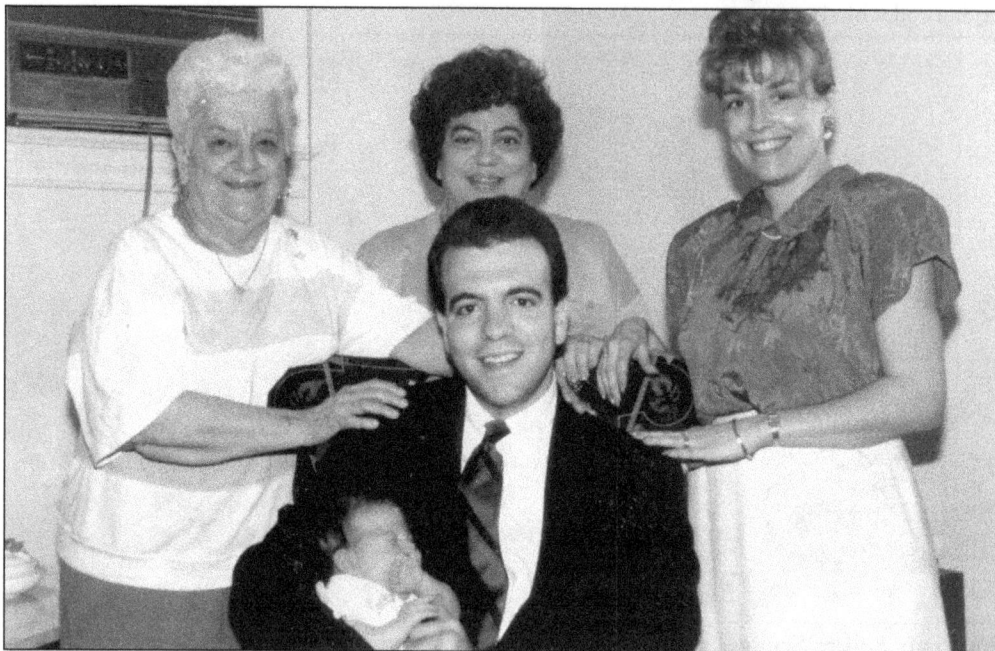

Lifelong resident Adeline Buzzelli Orsini beams with pride for grandson Dan Onorato after his election to Pittsburgh City Council in 1991. Dan, holding firstborn daughter Kate, is surrounded by, from left to right, grandmother Adeline; mother Vivian, a former schoolteacher at Immaculate Conception Catholic School; and wife Shelly. Daniel went on to become today's Allegheny County chief executive.

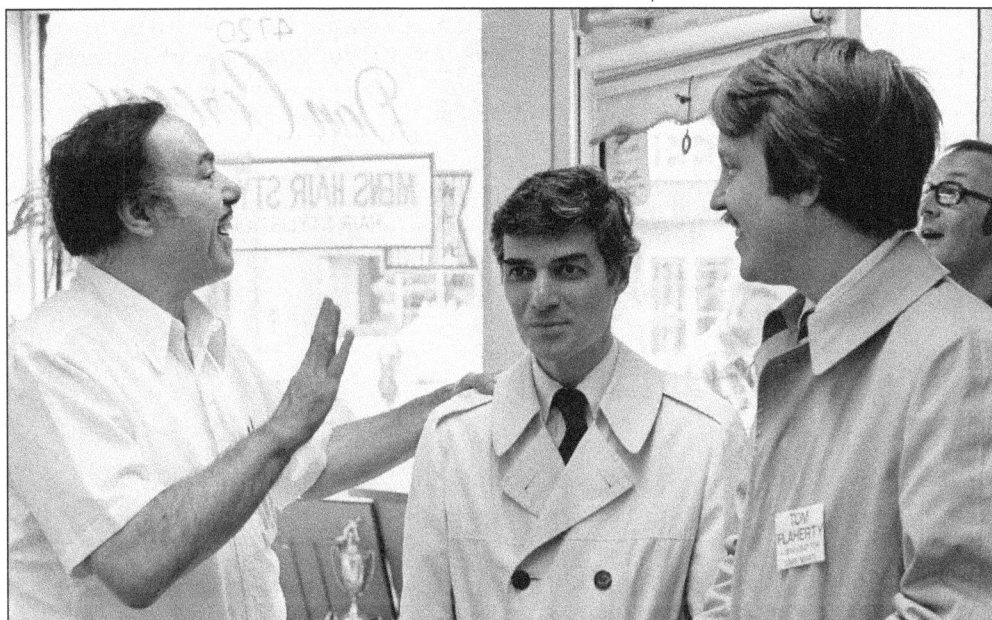

Dan Cercone, Bloomfield community leader/businessman, is pictured in a moment of taking charge with Pittsburgh mayor Dick Caliguiri and senate candidate Tom Flaherty in his barbershop. Cercone's hands say it all at a time when political pressures were rising. Flaherty lost the Democratic Party endorsement for senate by two votes to Leonard Bodack Sr. Flaherty is now a sitting judge.

In the 1980s, the Bloomfield Citizens Council worked on $1 million worth of capital improvements at Dean's Field for the youth of Bloomfield. New Astroturf, a hockey court, bocce court, Tot Lot, fencing, and lighting were the reason the entire town came out to thank Mayor Sofie Maslof (at center, cutting the ribbon) and Louise Brown (holding the ribbon), director of Bloomfield Parks and Recreation for their support and guidance.

Specialist E5 Angelo Tabuso served in the armed forces from 1968 to 1970 in the 4th Armored Division. He is a past commander of Bloomfield Catholic War Veterans Post 753.

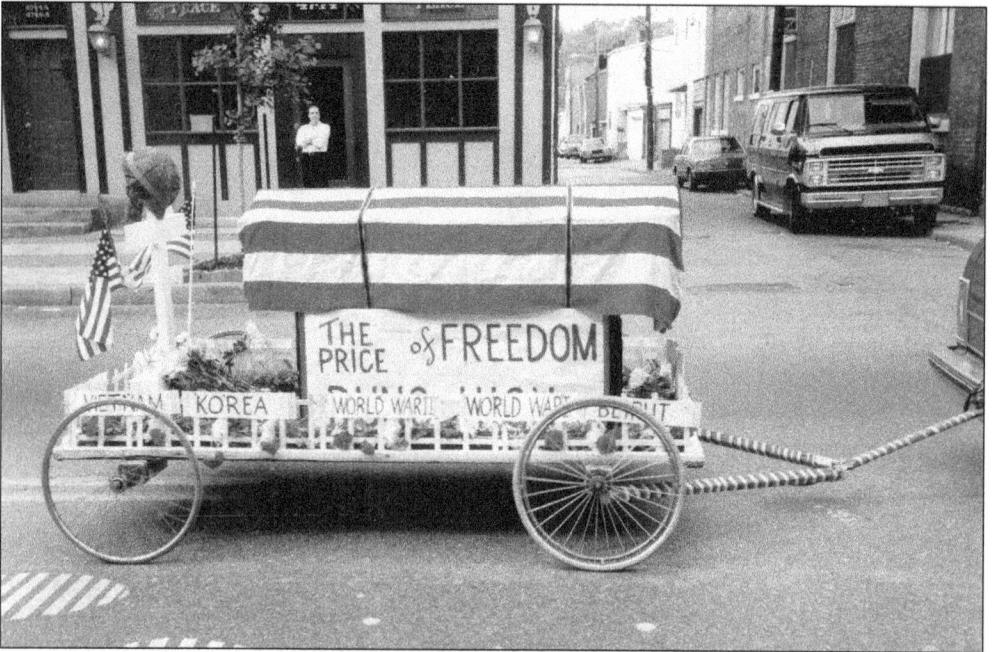

The VFW Jene-Mager Post 278 was vigorous and active in Bloomfield, supporting all community activities. This float was part of the Bloomfield annual Memorial Day parade when all local veterans marched from the war monument in Morrow Park through Bloomfield to the cemeteries on Penn Avenue.

Seven

A STRONG SENSE OF COMMUNITY

In the year 1990, Bloomfield received its most requested need as expressed by the people themselves. It was their desire to have their own neighborhood newspaper—one that would showcase Bloomfield's goodness.

After researching the possibility, the Cercone and Scullion families responded, with help from their friends, by publishing the first issue of the *Spirit of Bloomfield* family magazine. It has continued into the 21st century, carrying the seal of the Holy Spirit, circled by the words *education*, *truth*, *culture*, and *advocacy*, and gave birth to the Bloomfield Preservation and Heritage Society.

Continuously celebrating life and camaraderie, Bloomfield hosts Pittsburgh's largest nighttime Halloween parade; the Pittsburgh Marathon; an Italian festival; Arts in the Park; Church festivals; Little League and girls' softball through the spring, summer, and fall; the grand prix; and the Sons of Columbus Parade.

The 21st century started off with millions of dollars in investments in West Penn Hospital, Shadyside Hospital, Hillman Cancer Center, and Children's Hospital of Pittsburgh.

New private development, such as the Cercone Village on the Park and the Roma Building, has boosted the local economy with additional workforce and people to shop the avenue. It continues to be a multigenerational town with family-run and family-owned businesses.

Immaculate Conception Catholic School, Woolslair Public School, Waldorf private school, and numerous wonderful and reputable day care and nursery schools are providing quality education for children.

Walking the avenue is an experience in itself. There is a warm friendliness among the local gentry, architecture from the 1800s to dazzle the observer, shops and restaurants to please all tastes, and the projection of a high self-esteem and civic pride to the visitor. All in all, quite a lot of substance to develop a successful community.

Bloomfield examined what has been left behind by ancestors and that now is being used in modern times by the current population. It will also reveal the recipe for success in today's Pittsburgh's Little Italy.

The Bloomfield Sandlot Trojans football team lines up for a reunion under the Bloomfield Bridge with the Pittsburgh History and Landmarks photographer in 1991. From left to right, Robert Scullion Sr., Ben Mannella, Vincent Palmiere, Frank Guerriero, and Mickey Walton portrayed the "Men of Steel" on the field in the 1950s, 40 years before this photograph. Sports built friendships among the men that have lasted a lifetime.

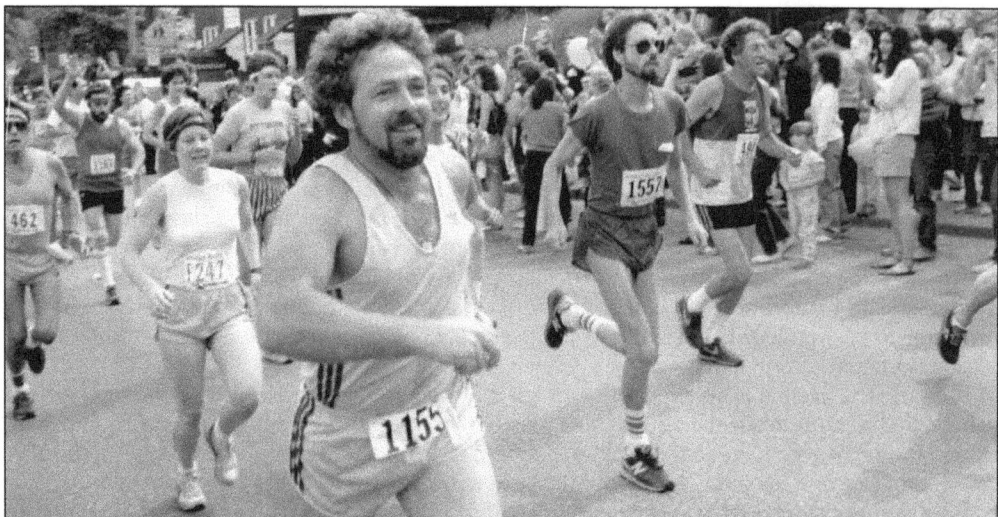

The Pittsburgh Marathon was hosted by the Bloomfield Citizens Council with water stations and live entertainment in Bloomfield, the 22nd mile of the 26-mile race for 16 consecutive years, until a temporary five-year hiatus. In 2009, the Pittsburgh Marathon resumes again and will run through Bloomfield, rated the No. 1 community by the runners themselves.

Enthusiasm for the Pittsburgh Marathon ran so high in Bloomfield even the three- and four-year-old children got in on the fun in the Bloomfield Citizens Council Walk-a-Thon in Friendship Park with T-shirts and balloons. The entire senior center membership, wearing the gift sun visors, would be the escort for the children. West Penn Hospital donated a free lunch for all.

Happy volunteers hand out cups of water during the race while lively music from a local disk jockey inspired Pittsburgh Marathon runners coming through Bloomfield. For 16 years, the Bloomfield Citizens Council manned two water stations on the 22nd mile of a 26-mile course. The Pittsburgh Marathon is returning on May 3, 2009, after a five-year absence.

The dedication of the Bloomfield girls' softball coach Eugene Zielmanski is unparalleled. Zielmanski (standing), shown with his All-State team and faithful coach Ed Wohlfiel (right), spent many evenings, Saturdays, and Sundays dedicated to the kids. Zielmanski and his wife, Barbara (not in picture), have over 34 consecutive years working for the youth of Bloomfield and the tristate area as well.

The Bloomfield Sports Hall of Fame is the result of grassroots athletes and youth baseball director Richard Romano. The gallery is in the lobby of Fidelity Bank at 4719 Liberty Avenue and contains special achievement awards that Romano's baseball league members have selected. Dan Brannigan was honored for work with Bloomfield youth basketball teams, which have been champions in the tristate area and the state of Pennsylvania often during his decade of service.

This very familiar sight of Pastor Fr. Domenic Oliveri enjoying life in Bloomfield with his parishioners was taken on a summer evening at the bocce court provided through Bloomfield Citizens Council funding efforts. Father Oliveri was given the title of the "people's priest" by the *Spirit of Bloomfield* family magazine.

The Bloomfield Women's Bocce League has given the men's league (top photograph) some tense moments at the end-of-the-season competitions. They have been known to outscore the men at the game, although this is a little-published fact.

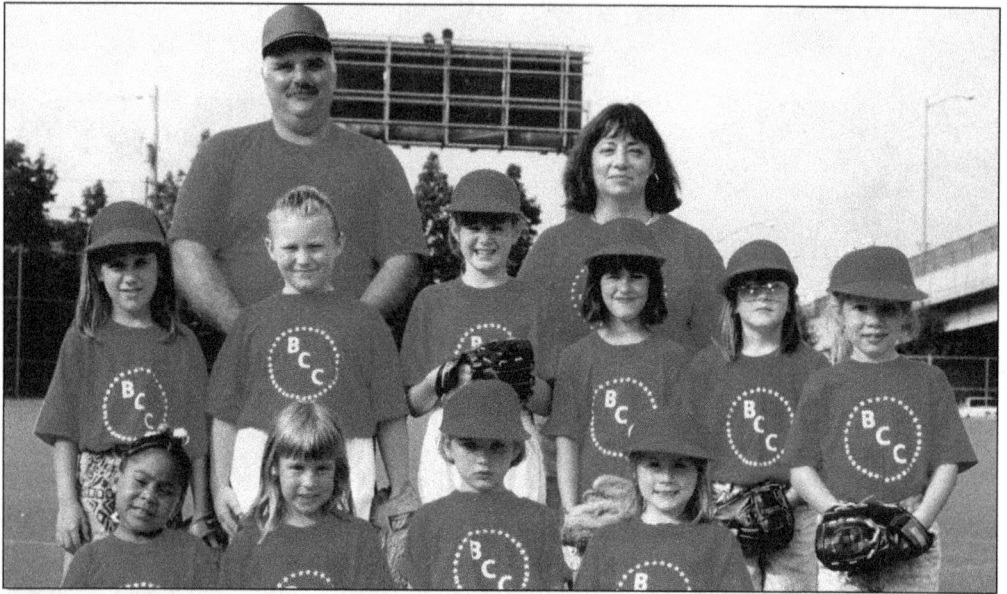

The Bloomfield Citizens Council girls' baseball team in 1993 was coached by board of directors member Linda Bruno Vacca. Linda and her parents, Steven and Virginia Bruno, are strong volunteers at church and school activities, showing up to work as a family. Lawrence Cammerota, standing left, is a community-service advocate and has coached youth baseball and football with the Pittsburgh Passions Women's Football League. He is a marshal for the Bloomfield Citizens Council Halloween Parade Committee.

Rose Larus (not shown), president of Senior Friends, Inc., has worked with the children of Bloomfield in the old-fashion sport of marbles, conducting weeklong tournaments at Immaculate Conception School. She has produced competition winners in national marble tournaments for over a decade.

The Bloomfield Catholic girls varsity team were winners of the basketball championship in 2001. Pictured from left to right are (first row) coach Brean Caldwell, Vincenza Tolomea, Ashlie Scullion, and Erin Hurrle; (second row) Carly Murphy, Liz Murello, Alycia Peraglia, Megan Burke, Liz McMahon, Kasey McMeekin, and coach T. R. O'Connor. Coach Angela Tolomeo and scorekeeper Robert Scullion Jr. are not pictured.

The Bloomfield Senior Center on Pearl Street, managed by Sr. Loralee (standing), provides immeasurable benefits to Bloomfield seniors that improve their quality of life. Mary Provenzano (seated, left) and Irene Weber show their handmade, award-winning afghan at the senior center headquarters. The companionship and sense of belonging are reflected in this photograph.

John T. Collinger, owner of the Pleasure Bar, left an indelible imprint on Bloomfield. The colorful Collinger legacy of brothers John, Samuel, Michael, Thomas, and William literally lit up the corner of Liberty Avenue and Cedarville Street with sports talk. John's wife, Thelma Reinsfelder Collinger, came from the family running the well-known Reinsfelder Trucking Company on Ella Street.

John Collinger's Pleasure Bar at Liberty Avenue and Cedarville Street continues to be a successful Bloomfield landmark in the 21st century, long after his passing in 1995. Modern-day owners James and Jamie Campau and Derek Bray, from the state of Michigan, continue to reap the benefits of the Collinger mystique. Seems everyone has been to the Pleasure Bar or knows where this building built in 1923 is located. It was and still is the hub of national sports action today.

Joseph "Buff" Carlino, standing next to the Honus Wagner statue, is the gifted granite cutter whose hands created the form of the children looking up at Wagner. The Milgate Street resident worked 62 consecutive years before he retired at age 83. The statue was sculpted by Frank Vittor and dedicated on April 15, 1955.

Dan Cercone (center) opened his barbershop in 1931 at the age of 18 with help from his parents Panfilo and Rachel Ciarelli Cercone. Dan became Hairstylist of the Year four times and invented the Concavex hairstyling shears that revolutionized the industry. Long hair for men became the rage in the 1960s and 1970s. Shown with Dan are his daughter Janet Cercone Scullion and son-in-law Bob Scullion Sr.

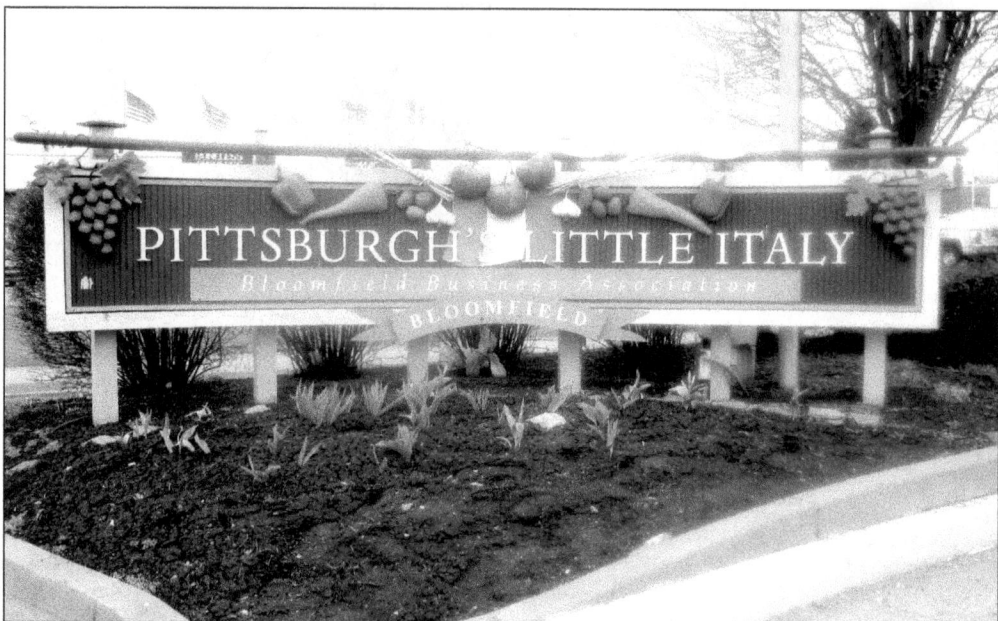

The Little Italy sign designation came through the efforts of the Bloomfield Business Association president Gloria LeDonne in July 1993. She was the first woman president of the organization and had a successful 10-year term as the person to hold the longest term in that office. A business directory, Snowflake Festival, Breakfast with Santa, spring festival, and instituting Little Italy Days were among her accomplishments.

Del's Restaurant and Bar, located at 4428 Liberty Avenue, was established in 1949 by Mary and Bernardino DelPizzo, Italian immigrants with roots on neighboring Larimer Avenue. Sons Robert and Dino joined in the family operation that would eventually move to the third generation of DelPizzo's today.

Paul Donatelli's father, Frank, started an Italian grocery store business in 1932 and was 15 years younger than his pierogi-smoking partner, the quiet George Rosato. They use the *Libretto* (book) to give credit to immigrant families for three and four generations. In 1960, Paul came into the business that is sustained by him and his wife Doris, his sons Paul Jr. and Russell, and son-in-law Greg Salac. They also live in Bloomfield.

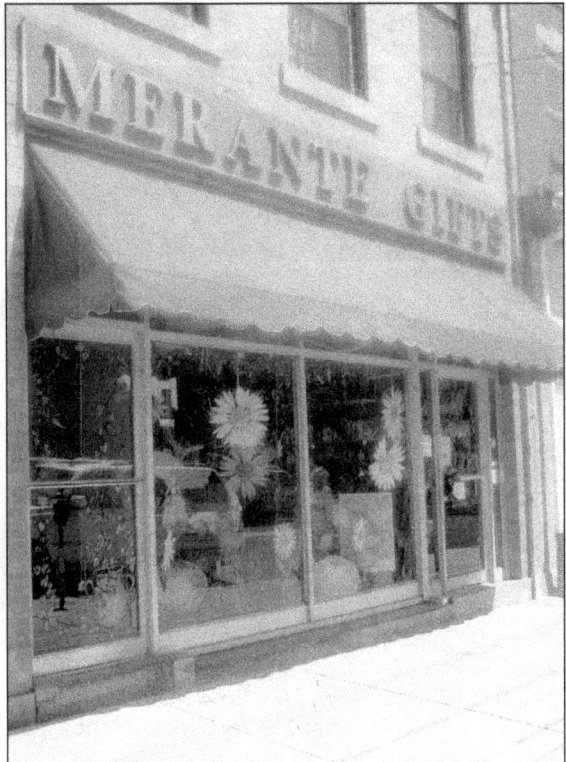

The Merante store at 4723 Liberty Avenue is a destination stop, attracting shoppers to Bloomfield from other states for unique one-of-a-kind ethnic items since 1995. Cooking classes, heritage-enrichment events, and conversational Italian classes are offered for the Merante experience.

Prosdocimo Matteo Donatucci had a promising career in baseball because of a wicked curve ball that earned him the lifetime name "Hooks." He played baseball with the famed Honus Wagner All-Stars in the 1930s and worked as a professional umpire as well. He never forgot his humble beginnings, being the eighth child of 15 children born to his immigrant parents, Guiseppe and Pasqualina Donatucci.

Groceria Italiana has established a strong presence in the Bloomfield community under the skillful culinary arts of owner Rose Marie Ricci, a former restaurant owner in Mount Lebanon. Her sons James and Joseph Luvara handle all the aspects of the business, creating what Bloomfield is known for—the family enterprise.

Maryann's Restaurant, at 4759 Liberty Avenue at the corner of Edmond Street, has been an intimate eatery owned and managed by Maryann Mori and son Rocky Mori long enough to become a Bloomfield landmark. Rocky's name has been on the awning since the 21st century and the restaurant remains a social hot spot.

Close family relationships have been the essence of Adelia Ricci's being since leaving Ateleta, Italy, in 1954. Her husband of one year, Guiseppe, traveled to Bloomfield in 1953 to save for her voyage six months later. He worked in construction as their daughter Maria and son Joseph were growing up, and together they achieved the American dream of owning a home. Today daughter Maria Fatta and granddaughter Laura perpetuate the closeness at Adelia's side.

Armand's Bar at 4755 Liberty Avenue has a reputation for serving the biggest and the best fish sandwich in town. Armand Lombardozzi came to America in 1959 from Roccacinquemiglia, Abruzzo, Italy. He bought the business from his brother Anthony in the 1960s and keeps a lot of social interaction going for the customer.

Lombardozzi's Restaurant, on the corner of 4786 Liberty Avenue and Mathilda Street, has clientele that travel from out of state for their traditional seven-course meal. Owner Anthony (Tony) Lombardozzi made his way to America from Roccacinquemiglia, Abruzzo, Italy, in 1954. In elegant style, Tony always greets his guests personally.

D'Amico's Place has been opened since 1983 and doubled in size 10 years later. Owner Frank D'Amico came to America in 1968 from Roccacinquemiglia, Abruzzo, Italy. The signature handmade pasta in its Italian dishes put the restaurant on the map as a Pittsburgh destination.

Alexander's Pasta Express at 5104 Liberty Avenue has been owned and operated by Alex Colaizzi's family for several decades, receiving multiple awards year after year. It is a favorite visitors' spot.

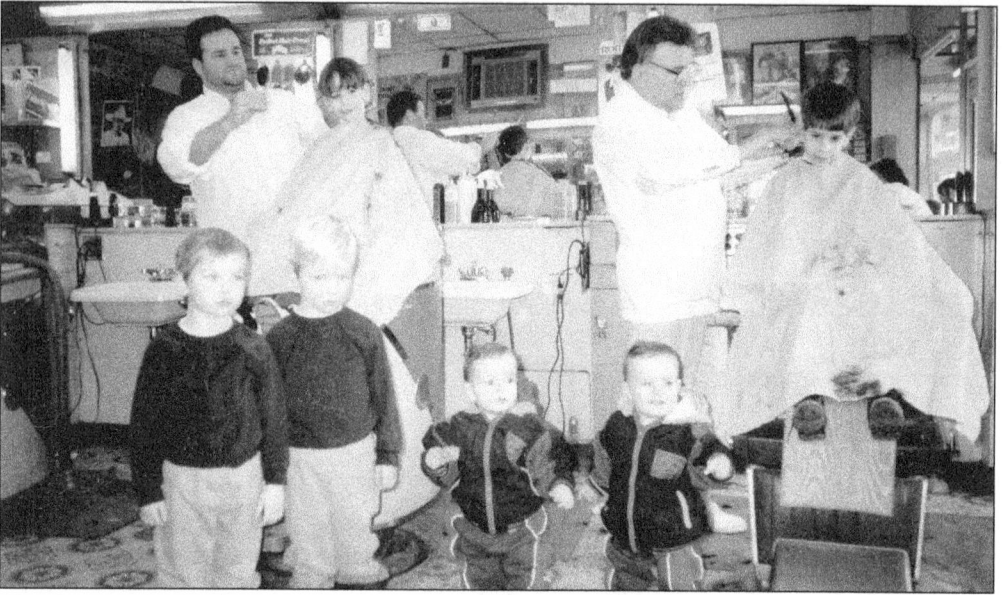

The Cercone barbershop is a well-known gathering spot for friends and families. On Saturday, February 3, 1996, Anthony Buzzelli Jr.'s 14-month-old twins, Brenden and Andrew, had finished getting their haircuts with barber and great-uncle Al Buzzelli (not shown), when Jay Carson arrived with his seven-year-old twins, Mackenzie and Jacob, shown with barber Dennis Scullion (left) and Steve Parvonik (right). The family gathering was punctuated with the entrance of Dominic Granata and his three-year-old twins, Dominic and Zachary.

The Giancola family could not be prouder than when John (center) received the Mary Cercone Outstanding Citizen Award for lengthy public service, and wife, Maffy, was selected for the Community Commitment Award by the Bloomfield Citizens Council, where John was past president and Maffey a board member. They work tirelessly with church organizations for all causes. Their children, from left to right, Linda, Anthony, and Nettie, are at their side in 2001.

Pharmacists James Koll (left) and Norman Talkowski (right) purchased the Bloomfield Drug Store in 1981 from druggist Bernard Danenberg. Judy Frizzi Koll (second from left) and Teresa Talkowski (third from left) actively participate in their husbands' bustling pharmacy, at 4727 Liberty Avenue at the corner of Cedarville Street, providing a rarely seen family theme with professional orientation. Judy's great-grandparents were immigrants from Abruzzo, Italy. Yost's Radio Store and Stiegerwald's Millinery occupied the space in the early 1920s.

Dr. Francesco Santucci, a first-generation American who speaks Italian fluently to his patients, has enhanced medical care in an ethnic neighborhood. Knowing everyone, since he was an altar boy at Immaculate Conception Church, football coach, and Little League coach in his hometown, put him in a position of great trust, in addition to his exceptional skills as a physician, and has created a rarity within a city neighborhood.

Fr. Richard Infante, a lifelong Bloomfield resident, provides the community with an evening with Dr. Sam Hazo, president and director of the International Poetry Forum. Dr. Hazo lived his boyhood in Bloomfield. Msgr. Charles Owen Rice, whose first priestly assignment was at Immaculate Conception Church, read an Irish verse. Theresa Barton (center) and Philip DeLuca (right) joined in at El Dolce Café for the memorable Bloomfield Arts Festival.

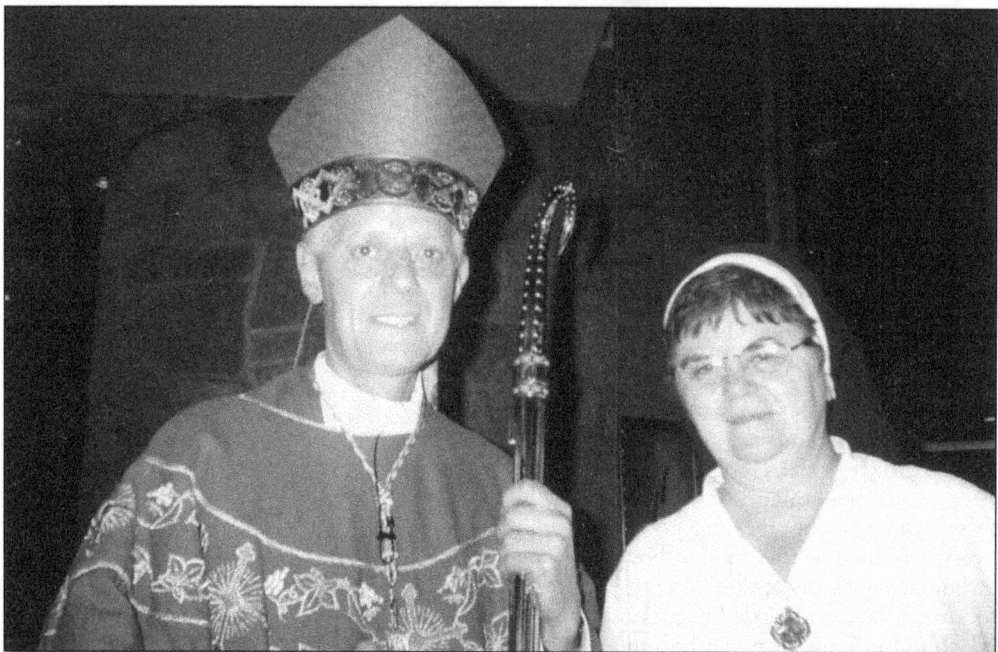

Sr. Mary John Cook shares a moment with Bishop Donald Wuerl during a visit to Immaculate Conception–St. Joseph Parish. In 2007, she celebrated 50 years as a sister of the Holy Spirit. She has been principal of Immaculate Conception School for 26 of those years and a teacher there for eight previous years.

As soon as William Dinello moved to Bloomfield, he joined the Bloomfield Citizens Council and started his own beautification project in the neighborhood. The octogenarian weeded and purchased bushes and flowers for the traffic light island at the entrance to the park on Friendship Avenue. A love of gardening and agriculture runs deep in the veins of villagers from Abruzzo, Italy, where his family has roots. Shown on the right is Robert Scullion Jr. who assisted Dinello with the project.

The new pastor Rev. John Dinello and Bishop Donald Wuerl celebrate his installation at Immaculate Conception–St. Joseph Parish in Bloomfield in August 2005.

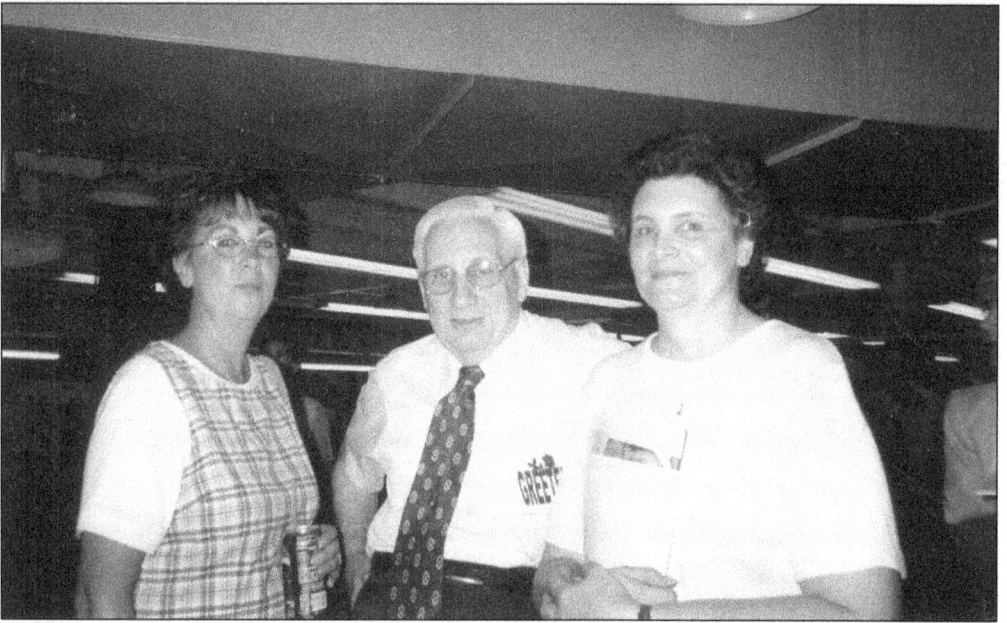

Joseph Niehaus is pictured with lifelong friends Debbie Nagy and Marlene Schimmel sharing one evening event at St. Joseph Church. Joseph Niehaus was the bell ringer at the church for decades before automation. He was an usher for over 50 years and still lives in his parents' home on Edmond Street. The Schimmel sisters, like Niehaus, are active in public service and continue to reside close to family in Bloomfield.

Pittsburgh councilman William Peduto (center) embraces and enjoys Irma and Elio Colazzi (left) and Anna and Vince Ricci (right) during an Italian-education program at the Bloomfield Preservation and Heritage Society Center. Councilman Peduto credits his grandfather from Abruzzo, Italy, who lived in his home, as being the one who taught him the importance of working hard to realize his dreams. He is very involved in heritage-advocacy issues.

Fr. John Dinello is pictured with Pittsburgh Diocese bishop David Zubik giving encouragement to seminarian Michael Gallagher regarding his future doing the work of the Lord. Gallagher and a group of seminarians participated in Lenten Stations of the Cross at Immaculate Conception–St. Joseph Parish followed by the Bloomfield Lenten custom of the parish fish fry dinner.

Congressman William Coyne is shown on the Capitol steps in Washington, D.C., in 2000 after the induction of the Bloomfield Preservation and Heritage Society's History and Architecture Educational Program for Children into the Library of Congress. Pictured from left to right are Janet Cercone Scullion, Karen Cercone, Vinessa Turpin, and Patty Ladasky.

On May 3, 1991, then a Pittsburgh city councilman, Jim Ferlo gave the keynote address at Woolslair School's federal designation as a historical landmark. This was a great honor for Woolslair School and Bloomfield from the United States Department of the Interior. Ferlo is now a Pennsylvania state senator known as a warrior for the cause of historic preservation. He is a first-generation Italian American with roots from Calabria, Italy, and he highly respects Bloomfield traditions.

Pennsylvania state representative Frank Pistella, 8th Ward Bloomfield (left), and Pennsylvania state representative Don Walko, 9th Ward Bloomfield (right), addressed 300 visitors at the Bloomfield Preservation and Heritage Society opening of the first exhibit center at 260 Edmond Street on September 8, 1999. Both elected officials have perpetuated preservation projects in Bloomfield and have Italian roots. Barry Deems, vice president of West Penn Hospital (second from left), and Patrick McGonagle, Bloomfield Preservation and Heritage Society Board of Directors member, participated in the event.

Bob O'Connor is shown at Bloomfield Citizens Council mayoral debate on May 10, 1997, with moderator Patti Burns. O'Connor faced off against Thomas Murphy, who won the election that year. On September 1, 2006, O'Connor passed away of brain cancer, six months after he achieved his dream of becoming mayor of Pittsburgh. Patti Burns, American journalist and television news anchor, preceded him in death by October 31, 2001.

History in the making
County Commisioner Larry Dunn and
City of Pittsburgh Mayor
Tom Murphy at
Bloomfield Preservation & Heritage Society
History Center

Pittsburgh mayor Thomas Murphy (right), Democrat, met with Allegheny County commissioner Lawrence Dunn, Republican, to discuss a strategy to focus on preservation and form an alliance with the Bloomfield Preservation and Heritage Society. They assisted with plans for an education program at the Heritage Center that ultimately achieved success and was inducted into the Library of Congress in 2000.

121

Louise Sturgess, Pittsburgh History and Landmarks executive director, is conducting historic preservation seminars for volunteers Margaret DelCimuto, Bina Shiring, Patricia Ladasky, and Joanne Lupone at the headquarters of Bloomfield Preservation and Heritage Society. The women were preparing architecture awareness classes for elementary school students.

Attorney Daniel Berger greets Dr. Francesco Santucci as Raymond Fern looks on while the men began preparing for a Bloomfield Preservation and Heritage Society Board of Directors meeting. Daniel Berger also served on the *Spirit of Bloomfield* family magazine advisory board from 1990 to 2008, when he lost his battle with cancer.

The entire village of Roccacinquemiglia is represented here during an ethic celebration in Bloomfield. Pictured from left to right are Ada Lombardozzi, Virginia Grilli, Mary Grilli, Dora Girdano, Bina Shiring, and Ornella D'Achille. Girdana and Shiring were volunteers at the Bloomfield Preservation and Heritage Society center.

From left to right, jovial Bloomfield Preservation and Heritage Society board members Patrick McGoingle, Karen Cercone, Philip Ciarelli, and guest Ruth Emmerling attended an Irish in America lecture at the Bloomfield History Center. All education programs at the center are free and open to the public.

Umberto Buccigrossi, a celebrity in his own right, points to wall photograph of the infamous Tom Savini, a make-up artist who crafted the monsters for George Romero's movie *Night of the Living Dead*. On the fence of his Taylor Street house, Savini has a ghoulish figure to greet visitors. Octogenarian Buccigrossi appeared on the David Letterman show because of Letterman's fascination with Buccigrossi's work as a cobbler for 75 years.

Congressman Michael Doyle was 49 years old when he began his fifth term in January 2003 during the restricting of District 14. He is seen here during a special moment with local gardeners Pasquale Lombardo (right) and Vincent Manella, both immigrants from Abruzzo, Italy. The congressman's maternal grandparents were also from Italy.

The love in the eyes and on the faces of this mother-daughter team made evident the kind of family spirit that exists in Bloomfield, as well as the love and respect they had for each other. Lena Caruso is shown with her mother, Anna Marie DeVito Caruso, on Anna Marie's 103rd birthday in 2005. They shared a home on Pearl Street until Anna Marie's passing on March 3, 2006, a few months before her 104th birthday.

The Bloomfield Senior Center began a chapter of the Red Hat Society calling themselves the American Beauties of Bloomfield. Today the Red Hat Society counts more than 800,000 members in 36,000 chapters in the United States. Officially they boast of being a distinguished group with no rules.

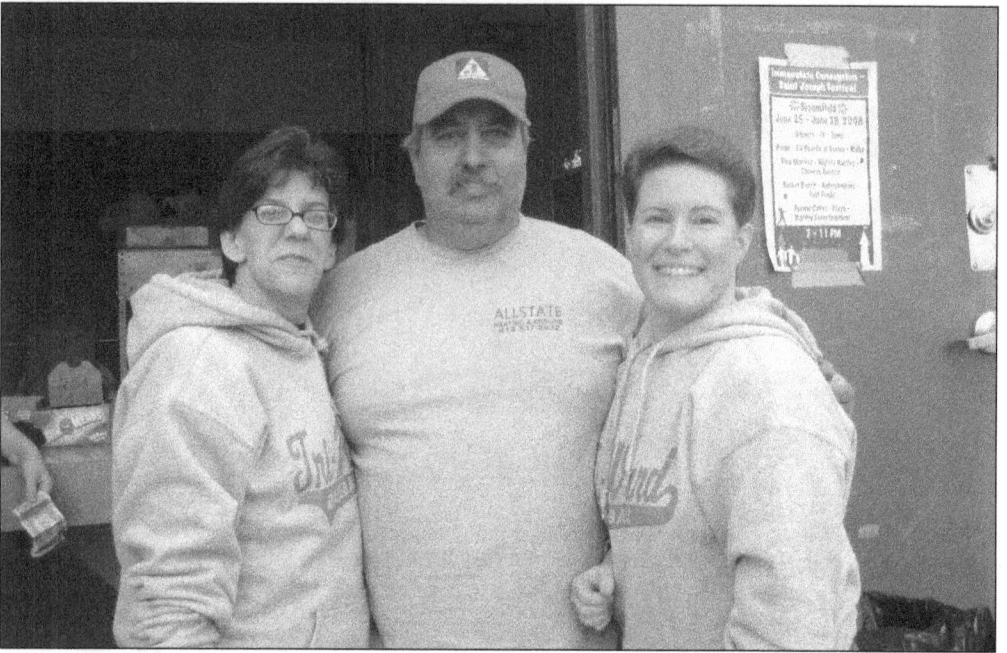

Bloomfielder's Sandra Tomasovich (left) and Corky and Mary McCabe manage the Tri-Ward Baseball League serving more than 160 families. They are shown at the grand opening of the state-of-the-art Dean's Baseball Field in June 2008. The three of them, with a large coaching and volunteer staff, are teaching children the true value of athletics.

This is a view of the new Dean's state-of-the-art baseball field in Bloomfield in 2008. It was the third major renovation secured by the Bloomfield Citizens Council in 40 years. The Bloomfield ball field is one of the most highly used facilities in the city of Pittsburgh.

126

This was a special night with Pittsburgh mayor Luke Ravenstahl (white shirt and tie) and the Bloomfield Citizens Council at the grand opening of newly renovated Dean's Baseball Field in 2008. Pictured from left to right are Anthony Sciullo, Emil DelCimuto, Janet Cercone Scullion, Patty Ladasky, Ida Czarnecki, Jean Mazzotti, Jane Foley, Phyllis McQuillen, and Jolene Brozi. Not pictured are council members Joseph Covelli and Linda Vacca.

The Cercone Village on the Park was erected in 2003 as a tribute to the immigrants of Bloomfield with a tower of light at the entrance, symbolizing hope for the future. Nine hundred residents of the community have their names inscribed on bricks in the Circle of Friends Courtyard in front of the building. The Bloomfield Preservation and Heritage Society headquarters is located in this building.

Visit us at
arcadiapublishing.com

www.ingramcontent.com/pod-product-compliance
Lightning Source LLC
Chambersburg PA
CBHW080600110426
42813CB00006B/1356